T. S. Eliot's Concept of Language

A Study of Its Development

Harry T. Antrim

University of Florida Press

Gainesville • 1971

821.912
An8I
99725
Jan. 1977

Acknowledgments

I AM GRATEFUL to Ants Oras, who read this in a much earlier version and made wise and useful suggestions, and to T. Walter Herbert, who read it in more recent form and encouraged its publication. I also want to express my appreciation to the Graduate School of the University of Florida for making this publication possible and to Donald Watson, of the University of Virginia, for his exacting and careful editorial assistance. And I must thank Henry T. Lilly and James S. Purcell for having introduced me to Eliot long before I ever thought about putting pen to paper.

Quotations from *Collected Poems 1909–1962, Selected Essays,* New Edition, *Essays on Elizabethan Drama, Murder in the Cathedral, The Cocktail Party,* by T. S. Eliot are reprinted by permission of Harcourt Brace Jovanovich, Inc.; copyright 1932, 1935, 1936, 1950, 1956, by Harcourt Brace Jovanovich, Inc., copyright 1950, 1960, 1963, 1964, by T. S. Eliot. Acknowledgment is also made to Farrar, Straus & Giroux, Inc., for permission to quote from T. S. Eliot, *Knowledge and Experience in the Philosophy of F. H. Bradley,* 1964, and to Methuen and Co. Ltd., for permission to quote from T. S. Eliot, *The Sacred Wood,* 1920. I am also grateful to Faber and Faber Ltd., for permitting me to quote at length from T. S. Eliot's published works.

Contents

Introduction

THERE ARE INDEED, things that cannot be put into words. They *make themselves manifest*. They are what is mystical."[1] It is not likely that T. S. Eliot ever read this, the final proposition of Ludwig Wittgenstein's *Tractatus Logico-Philosophicus*, but it is evident, I think, that the notion it expresses is pertinent to the position Eliot himself came to articulate late in his career. When he says in the *Quartets* that the "poetry does not matter,"[2] he is stating the same understanding about the relation between word and act, between word and expectation, and between word and reality that Wittgenstein, from another position, settles upon. For the philosopher, such a conclusion presents certain problems, but they do not necessarily undermine his habit of philosophizing.[3] For the poet, however, a similar realization raises questions which strike at the very center of his vocation, and for Eliot, the philosopher-turned-poet, the questions which issue from such speculation have special importance. The purpose of this study is to suggest some of the origins, in the early Eliot, of the conclusion that finally "the poetry does not matter" and to examine the changes in his concept of language wrought by the process of arriving at such a conclusion. If Eliot's poetic career begins in the heyday of British idealism in philosophy, it comes to a close at the time of

1. Ludwig Wittgenstein, *Tractatus Logico-Philosophicus*, trans. D. F. Pears and B. F. McGuiness (London, 1961), p. 151.

2. *The Complete Poems and Plays, 1909–1950* (New York, 1952), p. 132. Hereinafter, this title will be indicated in the text by *CP*. In addition, the following frequently cited works will also be indicated by abbreviations: *Selected Essays* (London, 1958), *SE*; *The Use of Poetry and the Use of Criticism* (London, 1933), *UPC*; *On Poetry and Poets* (New York, 1957), *OP*; *The Sacred Wood* (London, 1920), *SW*; *Collected Plays* (London, 1962), *P*; *Knowledge and Experience in the Philosophy of F. H. Bradley* (London, 1964), *KE*.

3. The *Tractatus* first appeared in 1921; shortly after, Wittgenstein repudiated most that it contained, spending the decade of the thirties formulating a new and more complete logic, which has appeared, since his death, from fragmentary notes kept by himself and his students.

1

great debate between the logical positivists and the newly arrived common language philosophers of Oxford and Cambridge. It is often remarked that ours has been a time of criticism, and this is just as true philosophically as literarily. That words can be made to reach across the void left by the disappearance of God (and hence of all Absolutes) and thereby re-establish some basis of relation with forms existing outside the subjective and ego-centered self has been one of the chief concerns of the first half of the twentieth century. Eliot, by denying the disappearance of God, discovers that language can be used to bridge the void and, then, to reaffirm the validity of a metaphysic. But the movement from the irony and self-isolation of a Prufrock to an affirmation of the *reality* of an incarnate Absolute has not yet been fully explored.

The direction of these essays has been largely suggested by two major examinations of nineteenth- and twentieth-century writers by J. Hillis Miller. In the first, *The Disappearance of God*, Miller sought to trace the recession of the spiritual horizon as it was expressed in the work of five nineteenth-century English poets and novelists; in the second, *The Poets of Reality*, he has attempted to show that one of the characteristic movements in recent poetry has been the reassertion of some sort of metaphysical *reality* outside the closed center of individual human cognition.[4] Miller's studies depend methodologically on the work of the French critic Georges Poulet, who examines the work of a particular writer as though it were all of one piece, focusing on its special habits of metaphor and image and probing its images of time and space in an attempt to illuminate the author's world-view. Up to a point, some of the method employed by these two critics is followed in this study, and there is great indebtedness to Miller's understanding of the aesthetic and philosophic milieu in which Eliot's poetry was written.

The Poets of Reality treats Yeats, Eliot, Thomas, Stevens, and W. C. Williams all as writers who, in their individual and various ways, begin with an experience of nihilism and move from that to assert a "new reality." Yeats achieves this, says Miller, "by his affirmation of the infinite richness of the finite moment; Eliot by his discovery that the Incarnation is here and now; Thomas by an acceptance of death which makes the poet an ark rescuing all things; Stevens by his identification of imagination and reality in the poetry of being;

4. The two books by J. Hillis Miller form, rather obviously, a sequence. It is to the initial chapters of the second that this study is most in debt.

Williams by his plunge into the 'filthy Passaic.' "[5] In spite of these different ways of achieving a vision of reality, all these five produce work in which "reality comes to be present to the senses, and present in the words of the poems which ratify this possession."[6]

Since the Incarnation is a making manifest of the remote and transcendent in the near and immediate through the revelation of God's grace in the Word, language is of critical importance to any belief in Incarnational reality. Any study of Eliot must therefore center on his understanding of language, its relational value, and its ultimate efficacy in presenting the mysterious union of subject and object, of God and creation. ("Here, the intersection of the timeless moment / Is England and nowhere. Never and always.") From the early ironic enclosure of Prufrock, locked within his own subjective ego, to the end of "Little Gidding," where "Every poem [is] an epitaph" and "the fire and the rose are one" (*CP*, 144–45), the course of Eliot's poetry, criticism, and drama is marked by a continuing attempt "to learn to use words" and a constant "raid on the inarticulate." The course of this struggle with language is further marked by a transition from involved and overt irony in the early poems to direct and (almost) prosaic statement in many of the later poems. Rather than having recourse to some mystical understanding, Eliot's poetry finally arrives at a level of incantation and contemplation where words take on the aura of sacramental gesture. If the Word has validity, then words, by analogy, have theirs, and even orthography can be relied upon as having a permanent value and meaning.

Belief in Incarnation enables Eliot to take hold of a world in which language is something other than what the mind makes of it. Language can be the means of both real communication and valid offering and thus may be especially useful when overtly public, as in the drama, which occupies Eliot increasingly after "Ash-Wednesday." The task of specifying the "impossible union" where "Spheres of existence [are] actual" and "past and future . . . reconciled" is not easily fulfilled, however, and is only accomplished after a number of false starts. But the materials for the final achievement are provided in the foundation, along with the impetus to make the effort. In the first chapter, I will suggest some of those original materials and point up some of the sources of Eliot's initial de-

5. Miller, *The Poets of Reality* (Cambridge, 1965), p. 11.
6. Ibid.

parture from the irony of Laforgue and the solipsism of F. H. Bradley. In the second chapter some attention will be given to Eliot's early experience with the problem of criticism and what it suggests to him about the nature and role of language, not only for the pursuit of literary and social critique, but for poetry and drama as well. In the last chapters I will examine the results of those early lessons as they take shape in the plays and the late poetry.

Throughout I have tried to remain conscious of the fact that what is being examined is not just a poem or a play but also a process. Eliot himself was aware of this as early as 1917, and the famous part of "Tradition and the Individual Talent" bears repeating:

> No poet, no artist of any art, has his complete meaning alone. His significance, his appreciation is the appreciation of his relation to the dead poets and artists. You cannot value him alone; you must set him, for contrast and comparison, among the dead. *I mean this as a principle of aesthetic, not merely historical, criticism.* The necessity that he shall conform, that he shall cohere, is not onesided; what happens when a new work of art is created is something that happens simultaneously to all the works of art which preceded it. The existing monuments form an ideal order among themselves, which is modified by the introduction of the new (the really new) work of art among them. The existing order is complete before the new work arrives; for order to persist after the supervention of novelty, the *whole* existing order must be, if ever so slightly, altered; and so the relations, propositions, values of each work of art toward the whole are readjusted; and this is conformity between the old and the new.   (*SE*, 15, italics mine)

Though Eliot was to modify this view, it remained throughout the basis of his insistence that one must read an author in his entirety. This is particularly true of Eliot, for his work describes clearly a kind of spiritual journey, and one needs to get all of it if he is to get any of it. And the idea of process itself is pertinent in another way, for one of the conclusions Eliot reaches is that "for us, there is only the trying."

It is that process, then, of "trying," of "an intolerable wrestle / With words and meanings," which I hope to illuminate by following the sources of the major movements of Eliot's career with language as it traverses a course from irony to contemplation.

1
The Romantic Inheritance

That is not what I meant at all.
That is not it, at all.

PRUFROCK'S CONDITION is familiar to any reader of the early Eliot and is the embodiment, in poetry, of the result of certain ways of thinking which antedate Prufrock by at least two hundred and fifty years. The condition is the quintessence of subjectivity. Prufrock, perhaps never leaving the room of his own mind, finds his "life" measured "out with coffee spoons" and believes there is "time yet for a hundred indecisions, / And for a hundred visions and revisions, / Before the taking of a toast and tea." In such an atmosphere what visions there are for Prufrock are elusive and shifting, losing any possible objectivity in the ironic situation created by Prufrock's own thinking. Language itself is enmeshed in subjectivity and words take on a strangely disembodied character, informing here, "Streets that follow like a tedious argument / Of insidious intent," and there, "hands / That lift and drop a question on your plate." Little wonder that Prufrock finds it "impossible to say just what [he] mean[s]." He embodies Eliot's assertion that there is a "circle described about each point of view" (*KE*, 141).

The irony of Prufrock's circumstance derives from the constituents of his enclosed world ("the novels," "the teacups," and "the skirts that trail along the floor"); figments of his imagination, they appear real in some external sense as well. Reality "exists only through its appearance" and since that very idea is itself appearance, Prufrock finds it difficult "to maintain that there is any world at all, to find any objects for these mirrors to mirror" (*KE*, 202). Being itself subjectivized, language can communicate, ultimately, with no one but its user. All human potential and the world itself are locked within the confines of the word, and language reveals the agonizingly private nature of each experience and, hence, each individual.

5

It is a witless game to find the whole of a tradition or a course in history reflected or generated by one utterance, but it is nonetheless true that some assertions have had the effect of irrevocably altering the shape of man's conceptual world. The shape of Prufrock's conceptual world really begins to take form with Descartes and his radical formulation, *cogito, ergo sum*. The Dante whom Eliot had read by 1916 could not have found much meaning in Descartes' dictum, but the French poet Laforgue, whom Eliot had clearly absorbed by that same year, depends on that dictum just as surely as does Eliot himself.[1] Between the two, Dante and Laforgue, a world of phenomenal reality gives place to a world of mental projection. Setting man's cognition at the very center of the world, making it, in time, the creator of that world, leads to the aesthetic contretemps which Prufrock is an image of, and produces (in a complex of events) the philosophical currents which most profoundly affected Eliot, and did so at the most impressionable point in his career.

Eliot entered Harvard in 1906. Herbert Howarth, in *Notes on Some Figures Behind T. S. Eliot*, collects some contemporary impressions of the Harvard of those years and from them generalizes: "It was Harvard's golden era. At the beginning of this century William James was lecturing; Santayana; Royce; Babbitt; Kittredge; and others who, if their names have sounded less persistently across the world, were almost equally royal. Great teachers, intellectual athletes with a zest for many branches of knowledge, were training their students to their own versatility."[2] Of these figures Royce and Santayana were to have a special importance for the young Eliot; it was through Royce, initially, that Eliot came to be exposed to the prevailing idealist tendencies in the philosophical circles of the time—those which, in turn, were to lead him to a close examination of F. H. Bradley. As for his reading of poets, we have his own word that the ancients occupied him a great deal while contemporary English and American writers were not even known to him in 1906:

1. Eliot apparently began to read Dante sometime in 1911 after his return to Harvard from his year at the Sorbonne. He worked over the Italian with a translation before him and thus learned the language while steeping himself in Dante. See Herbert Howarth, *Notes on Some Figures Behind T. S. Eliot* (London, 1965), p. 74, and Kristian Smidt, *Poetry and Belief in the Work of T. S. Eliot* (London, 1961), p. 11. Eliot's discovery of Symons, and thereby Laforgue, is recalled in some remarks in the *Criterion*, January, 1930, p. 64.
   2. P. 64.

Whatever may have been the literary scene in America between the beginning of the century and the year 1914, it
remains in my mind a complete blank. I cannot remember the
name of a single poet of that period whose work I read; it was
only in 1915, after I came to England, that I heard the name
of Robert Frost. Undergraduates at Harvard in my time read
the English poets of the '90s, who were dead; that was as near
as we could get to any living tradition. Certainly I cannot
remember any English poet then alive who contributed to my
own education. Yeats was well-known, of course, but to me,
at least, Yeats did not appear, until after 1917, to be
anything but a minor survivor of the '90s. (After that date I
saw him very differently. . . .) . . . there was no poet, in either
country, who could have been of use to a beginner in 1908.
The only recourse was to poetry of another age and to poetry
of another language.[3]

As is now well known, the other age was the nineteenth century
and the other language was French. In 1908 Eliot read Symons'
The Symbolist Movement in Literature, which, as he later remarked,
appeared to him "as an introduction to wholly new feelings, as a
revelation" (SW, 5). "But for having read his book," he says, "I
should not, in the year 1908, have heard of Laforgue or Rimbaud;
I should probably not have heard of Corbière. So the Symons book
is one of those which have affected the course of my life" (SW, 6).

Indeed, it was in the French Symbolists that Eliot discovered
some possibility of a new poetry. Of those writers whom Symons
surveys in the edition of 1908 (Gerard de Nerval, Villiers de
L'Isle-Adam, Rimbaud, Verlaine, Laforgue, Mallarmé, Huysmans,
Maeterlinck), it was Laforgue Eliot found most intriguing.[4]

Laforgue's practice is but a natural development from the notion
that all we have by which to figure forth the world is our own
speech; and when that leads to a feeling that the world is *only*
our own saying it, then the result is likely to be an extreme self-
consciousness. Any extreme consciousness of self, in poetry, is likely
to prompt a heightened sense of irony.

Had Eliot's chief interest in 1908 been poetry rather than philosophy, he might have then steeped himself in Laforgue and pro-
ceeded to imitate his ironic view, thinking that by so doing he was

3. "Ezra Pound," *Poetry*, 68 (September, 1946): 329.
4. "Talk on Dante," *Italian News*, 2 (July, 1950): 16.

achieving a similarly "new" poetry in his own language, but Eliot was then more interested in philosophy. And it is, I think, from out of the combination of poetry and philosophy, and particularly the stylistic features of both in the kinds he read, that the figure of Prufrock emerges. That singularly enigmatic figure is the poetic embodiment of the sensitive soul confronted by the epistemological dilemma of the day. Prufrock is fashioned out of those strains which, for the Eliot of 1908–14, are best represented in the philosophizing of F. H. Bradley and the poetizing of Laforgue. The idea of Laforgue's poetry and the style of Bradley's philosophy point to the same thing: a world of mind is an enclosure continually reverted to in the utter privacy of the self. For the philosopher, such a world is always threatening to become merely a linguistic trap; for the poet, such a world is a place of profound pessimism where the only human posture is an ironic view of one's self.

The important effect of Bradley upon Eliot the poet is through his style of thought. Certainly he could not have presented to the Eliot of those years a way markedly different from the course which Laforgue figures forth in his poetry. Much has been made of Bradley's influence on Eliot, and the effect of those by whom Bradley, in his own turn, was influenced, and several perceptive critics have carefully traced the persistence of certain Bradleyan ideas in Eliot's poetry.[5] But there has been, I think, a tendency to overestimate the importance of Bradley in one sphere with the result of not realizing his importance in another. I have in mind here the critical distortion of treating Eliot's poetry and drama as chiefly the thinly veiled repository of philosophical ideas and the naturally resulting practice of extracting the philosopher from the verse. That Bradley (and other thinkers, for that matter) are important to Eliot goes without saying now, but the way in which Bradley had an effect is yet to be fully explored. Eliot's own late recollection of Bradley's value to him might suggest that his style of statement alone is worth more

5. The earliest study treating Eliot's work on Bradley is R. W. Church, "Eliot on Bradley's Metaphysic," *Harvard Advocate,* 125 (December, 1938): 24–26. More recently, a number of critics have devoted space to the influence of Bradley on Eliot's development. Eric Thompson, *T. S. Eliot—The Metaphysical Perspective* (Carbondale, 1963), is the only book which makes Bradley a major focus for examining Eliot's work, but among some numerous incidental mentions of Bradley the following are of value: Smidt, *Poetry and Belief,* pp. 158–63; Sean Lucy, *T. S. Eliot and the Idea of Tradition* (London, 1960), pp. 139–41; Hugh Kenner, *The Invisible Poet* (New York, 1959), pp. 11–14.

study than it has been granted. At the very least, Bradley informs the early Eliot in more ways than the exclusively ideational.

But first, Bradley's thought: whence did it come and what sort of position did it articulate? It is fair to assume that Eliot's introduction to Bradley came through Royce, whom Eliot once called "that extraordinary philosopher."[6] Royce was a monist and a post-Kantian idealist who held the whole universe to be contained in an all-comprehensive Mind, the Logos, or the Absolute, and be differentiated within that Mind into individuals—human, organic, and "inanimate." It was essentially a voluntaristic philosophy, stressing the ability of the individual to work out his salvation by an effort of the will pursued within the grace afforded by the Community. Because of this, Royce put a great deal of emphasis on the value of loyalty and on the inherent value to be found in both order and security.

But it was with Bradley that Eliot spent most of his time, reading (probably under Royce's guidance) his *Ethical Studies* (1876), *The Principles of Logic* (1885), and *Appearance and Reality* (1883). The impetus of much of Bradley's work was negative, centering on a continuing attack upon the British Empiricists. Drawing on the work of Hegel and Lotze, Bradley struck at the Empiricist doctrine of Mind and Inference, finding their "psychologism" the weakest link in their chain of logical postulation: "In England at all events we have lived too long in the psychological attitude."[7] His main point against the Empiricists could be summed up by saying that "he objected to their interpretation of the thesis that philosophy is the study of human knowledge or thought."[8] What for the Empiricists came to be regarded as an *idea* (basic unit of thought) Bradley asserted to be mere illusion and appearance. Where the Empiricists insisted upon the verifiable reality attendant on the image we form in our minds of any object, Bradley maintained, through a complicated epistemological critique, that such images were themselves appearances. To make them the object of empirical study was to assume they were existent, observable, verifiable phenomena. This, Bradley felt, was inherently wrong, for it led to a confusion between the phenomenalistic study of mind and the philosophical investigation of the objects of mind themselves.

6. "Introduction" to *Savonarola* (London, 1926), p. viii.
7. *Principles of Logic* (New York, 1912), p. 4.
8. Richard Wollheim, *F. H. Bradley* (London, 1959), p. 26.

But Bradley did not reject the possibility that even appearance exists in some respect; in fact, his major work, *Appearance and Reality*, is devoted to showing just how and in what way appearances exist and to what degree they constitute a portion of the truth we can know about Reality. It is at this point that Bradley's idealism becomes most evident, for here he argues that appearance, existing in some sense and forming part of Reality, needs only to be completed in a transcendent pattern to become fully real. Ethics and morals subscribe to the same understanding and thus even pain and evil have a place in a transcendent pattern, being finally encompassed by it and thereby transformed into good.

Yet Bradley's Absolute is not a Platonic vision of transcendencies; his universals give way (since no true universals can be other than concrete) to an all-embracing Universal—the world as a whole, or the Absolute.[9] It is almost as though Bradley were sitting astride a fence separating extreme idealism on the one side from extreme realism on the other. This precarious predicament led him to postulate degrees of truth, or degrees of appearance. This life is one of Appearance, because each mind is enclosed within itself. The Absolute (which is none other than the world itself) can only be apprehensible in its concrete form through the efficaciousness of what Bradley called "finite centers" (akin to Leibniz' monads), where all consciousness is contained in closed units complete in themselves and yet united in the Absolute. Bradley's rhetoric works mightily to carry the baggage of the argument and at times makes it appear as if he had indeed solved the problems inherent in postulating the unity of subject and object. There is nothing extreme about Bradley's position in these matters; instead, there is a sort of grandeur in his exposition of them which bespeaks an urbane, catholic mind rather than a narrow, dogmatic one.

Eliot may have been early attracted by that catholicity in Bradley and certainly such an attraction is part of his admiration of the man's style. In his 1927 essay on Bradley, Eliot remarks that "one of the reasons for the power he still exerts, as well as an indubitable claim to permanence, is his great gift of style." He goes on to compare Bradley's style to Arnold's for what, I believe, is an important, though usually overlooked, reason. Both men were, he notes, waging war against the same enemy—one which in Arnold's vocabulary

9. Ibid., p. 3.

was called Philistinism and in Bradley's, Utilitarianism. The weapons they each employed were the same: a close attention to and scrupulous use of words. They both wanted precision and they wanted it in the cause of a broadened perspective on the world of thought and ideas rather than in the effort to narrow the world down to compartments of particular usefulness. Both were, in this respect, antiscientistic. Eliot locates both Arnold and Bradley in what he calls "the Greek tradition" on the basis of their particular use of language. "Bradley," says Eliot, "like Aristotle, is distinguished by his scrupulous respect for words. . . . The tendency of his labors is to bring British philosophy closer to the Greek tradition."

The problem of language, though often obscured in Bradley's philosophizing, is central to that philosophizing, and Eliot's extended critique of Bradley taught him something both of the difficulty of saying what one really means and of the necessity of finding a view of reality which would permit saying anything at all.

In the conclusion to Eliot's dissertation on Bradley two observations stand out. Of the thing called "immediate experience" Eliot almost reluctantly concludes that it is a "paradox in that it means to be absolute, and yet is relative; in that it somehow always goes beyond itself and yet never escapes itself." And later, "the process toward the theoretical goal returns upon itself. We aim at a real thing: but everything is real as experience, and as thing everything is ideal" (KE, 166, 167). Finally, says Eliot, "Metaphysical systems are condemned to go up like a rocket and come down like a stick" (KE, 165). The only sure conclusion is to acknowledge that there is a distinction to be made between the practical and the theoretical and that on the basis of such a distinction a metaphysic may be accepted or rejected without assuming that from a practical point of view it is either true or false. Knowledge is relative and its relativity, concludes Eliot, is what "impels us toward the Absolute" (KE, 169). But in spite of the course Eliot's life was to take we cannot suppose that, in 1915, he had any idea of the shape that Absolute would take. For the time being, just having wrestled with Bradley and seen the paradox inherent in his thought was certainly instructive enough. In like manner, we should understand the implications of Eliot's conclusions regarding Bradley at the time he reached them and not be easily led to assume a complete acceptance of the master on the part of the disciple. True, Bradley's idealism (or idealism generally) never utterly disappears from Eliot's perspective, and we can note in advance that Christianity is always on the brink of plunging into one sort of idealist position or another. Nonetheless, Kenner, for one, is more polemical than right in asserting that the 1916 thesis "is evidence for his unqualified ingestion of certain perspectives of Bradley's which one does not discover him ever to have repudiated."[10]

If it cannot be maintained with ease that Eliot appropriates the *ideas* in *Ethical Studies* and *Appearance and Reality*, then what did Eliot gain from Bradley and why are we justified in reconsidering the question of Bradley's influence? The answer to the first question has already been suggested but will stand some elaboration, and the answer to the second follows from the first simply because those critics who have seriously considered Bradley have done so almost exclusively in terms of his philosophical position, paying little attention to the language in which it is so often couched and which Eliot appropriates in his critique of Bradley.

However closely related paradox and irony are, it would be far too facile to say that Eliot learns the force of the former from Bradley and of the latter from Laforgue, but such a gross oversimplification will serve as a point of departure and as an exaggeration to be modified. Paradox is not an inherent feature of idealisms, but for any idealist who focuses upon point of view, the latent possibility of rendering idealist positions paradoxical is likely to be realized. For the early followers of Descartes (they were oddly misnamed rationalists) the defense of the idealism implicit in his thought was not so difficult as it now might appear. Between Descartes and Bradley a world had changed, and some results of that change made the burden of defending Mind a heavy one indeed. Bradley's defense begins by rejecting the Cartesian derivation of everything from the experience of the self. His "immediate experience" is prior to any thinking or sensing. Descartes' "I" had become just another of the many appearances flesh is heir to and stands as proof that it is alienated from fundamental reality.

This essential paradox, revealed so clearly in Bradley's rhetoric, is also the paradox of Eliot's more general Romantic inheritance. From the aesthetic assumptions of the early nineteenth century, particularly in England and France, issues a potential dilemma as well as a new poetic freedom; the replacing of a hierarchical, cor-

10. Kenner, p. 45.

respondent world with one of Mind and its creative faculty, Imagination, releases the poet from bondage to the idea of transcendent Absolutes, but also cuts him off from the order and security which belief in such Absolutes affords.

As Hillis Miller points out, in a brilliant analysis of the problem, "romantic literature presupposes a double bifurcation." It divides existence into two realms, "heaven and earth, supernatural and natural, the 'real' world and the derived world. It is also divided into subjective and objective realms."[11] In the midst of that divided world man opposes himself, in his subjectivity, to everything else. Some romantic writers attempted, through poetry, to reunite subject and object by straining to locate God in the object, discovering him "A motion and a spirit, that impels / All thinking things, all objects of all thought / And rolls through all things."[12] But as one comes forward in the century, he is increasingly disabused of any hope in Absolutes actually being in Nature and comes finally to mourn, with Arnold, the retreating "sea of faith."

If the Absolute recedes far enough, then it is but a short step to the declaration that Absolutes do not exist. Thus, God is discovered to be dead. The death of God is one of the consequences of the attitudes inherent in Descartes' radical doubt, those attitudes nourished by the aesthetic assumptions of the early nineteenth century and, at the same time, themselves dependent on Descartes' formulation of self. God's demise also precedes Bradley and in so doing makes Bradley's paradox both possible and profound. Were Absolutes still existent, it would be childishly irresponsible to question that we can know them. A world once given objective reality through its sustenance in God's creativity has had its limits restricted to define a place where only man's egocentric self is the creator of all things. Man had, as Nietzsche both feared and exulted, "drunk up the sea":

"Where is God gone?" he called out. "I mean to tell you! *We have killed him,*—you and I! We are all his murderers! But how have we done it? How were we able to drink up the sea? Who gave us the sponge to wipe away the whole horizon? What did we do when we loosened this earth from its sun? Whither does it now move? Whither do we move? Away from

11. *Poets*, p. 1.
12. Wordsworth, "Tintern Abbey," *Complete Poems* (Cambridge, 1904), p. 91.

all suns? Do we not dash on unceasingly? Backwards, side-
ways, forewards, in all directions? Is there still an above and
below? Do we not stray, as through infinite nothingness? Does
not empty space breathe upon us? Has it not become colder?
Does not night come on continually, darker and darker? Shall
we not have to light lanterns in the morning? Do we not hear
the noise of the grave-diggers who are burying God? Do we
not smell the divine putrefaction?—for even Gods putrefy! God
is dead! God remains dead! And we have killed him!"[13]

God's death leaves man alone at the center of the world and
though for a moment the freedom gained is exhilarating, the conviction that man "is master of [his] fate" and "captain of [his]
soul"[14] breaks rapidly into a serious wistfulness and sense of loss.

Bradley grew up when various attempts were being made to as-
suage the loss of the Absolute, the death of God, and he himself
tries to exorcise the frightening void in a systematic metaphysic.
But what I have chosen to call the "romantic inheritance" questions
systems and metaphysics both, and Bradley is forced to reflect, in
words Eliot quotes in the notes to *The Waste Land*, that "regarded
as an existence which appears in a soul, the whole world for each
is peculiar and private to that soul."[15] The privacy of the self also
bespeaks the privacy of language and the French and English air
of the late nineteenth century is filled with literary programs advo-
cating private language as a necessary condition of true "poetry."

But it is significant that of the poets Symons introduced Eliot to,
it was to Laforgue and not Mallarmé that Eliot was attracted.
Language had to be private or if possible made so to suit Mallarmé's
conditions; for Laforgue, there is still the chance of saying something in a public way. In that respect, Laforgue and Bradley are
kin, for certainly the philosopher could have concluded that metaphysical probing only took him further away from the goal of the
Absolute and, so concluding, fallen silent. Rather than that, however, he took refuge in his paradoxical utterances, coming back
again to contemplate the relativity inherent in points of view. Depending upon the critic's point of view, Bradley's paradoxes them-

    13. Nietzsche, *The Joyful Wisdom,* trans. Thomas Common (London,
1918), Bk. III, sec. 125.
    14. William Henley, "Invictus," *Poems* (New York, 1910), p. 119.
    15. Bradley, *Appearance and Reality* (London, 1908), p. 346.

selves could be read ironically, but it has to be assumed that their originator never felt them so. Nonetheless, they may go a long way to enforcing a sense of irony in a young man already fascinated by a poet like Laforgue, and if that is true, then Bradley offers Eliot a philosophical and logical experience of the mind entrapped in its own ego-centered circle. That is quite another thing from providing a metaphysical basis for a long poetic career.

If Bradley is the careful and cautious philosopher tempering his idealism with paradox, Laforgue is the committed but mordant poet asserting his idealism behind the mask of irony. The two are contemporaries, Laforgue writing most of his major verse in the same two decades of Bradley's most significant production.[16] But they are contemporaneous in ways other than chronological, and though they did not know each other (at least, it is highly improbable that Bradley ever read any of Laforgue's poetry and even less likely that Laforgue ever became aware of Bradley's philosophy), they were both influenced by similar or parallel intellectual traditions.

Laforgue was enamored of Schopenhauer and, it would seem, took the latter's "the world is my idea" as the basis of his own position. Though Schopenhauer's ego-centered restatement of Descartes' *cogito* has varied implications for his own philosophical development, it was for Laforgue but a metaphysical redaction of what he more or less poetically intuited. For the early Laforgue, there is no object without a subject, nothing real but at the moment of its being perceived. Man dreams his world into being ("L'homme, ce fou rêveur d'un piètre mondicule . . .") and speaks to the earth which harbors him as though it would fall into nothingness were it not humanly perceived:

> C'était un songe, non! oui, tu n'as jamais été!
> Tout est seul! nul témoin! rien ne voit,
> Rien ne pense. . . .[17]

Such a vision is enough to impel a great sense of aloneness, and of being burdened by the responsibility of thinking of the world as more than mere atoms:

16. Though much of Laforgue's work was published after his death in 1887, the decade of the eighties was his most active period, as it was for Bradley.
17. Jules Laforgue, *Poésies complètes* (Paris, 1956), p. 27. An excellent study of Laforgue and his time is Warren Ramsey, *Jules Laforgue and the Ironic Inheritance* (New York, 1953).

Dans l'infini criblé d'éternelles splendeurs,
Perdu comme un atome, inconnu, solitaire,
Pour quelques jours comptés, un bloc appellé Terre
Vole avec sa vermine aux vastes profondeurs.[18]

That cold isolation is close to the nihilism which may result when-
ever subject and object are found to dissolve into meaningless
terms cast up out of the recesses of the encompassing self.

It was either such a realization or one akin to it which impelled
Laforgue to reach beyond the chilly pessimism of the early Schopenhauer and to explore the possibilities of self-negation and self-
denial. Confronted by nothingness and verbal ennui, one may come
to objectify some aspect of the world by suffering its remoteness:

Je n'ai fait que souffrir, pour toute la nature,
Pour les êtres, le vent, les fleurs, le firmament,
Souffrir par tous mes nerfs, minuitieusement,
Souffrir de n'avoir pas d'âme encore assez pure.[19]

Laforgue's experience with self-renunciation may remind us of
something similar in Eliot's career. At least, such reflections of it as
there are in Laforgue's poetry would not have escaped the attention
of his young American disciple. But it was largely the irony and the
pessimism in the French poet which impressed Eliot and it was
especially important to Eliot to see how Laforgue made the life
around him, the scenes of the city and the speech of its inhabitants,
the material of that irony. That Laforgue saw incongruities in the
daily scene more readily than most is testified to even in his most
prosaic moments, as when he describes Taine in the classroom:
"Taine's course.—His ridiculous trousers, too short, with a marked
bagging at the knees.—Rich in facts. For an hour one is transported
to the multifarious Italy of the sixteenth century. I look at the bent
skulls of the attentive auditors, on which light falls from above, with
nuance, February pale. These people are chewing marshmallow
creams, they have neckerchiefs, rubbers on their feet, flannels, um-
brellas. They are listening to the memoirs of Cellini, the lives of the
Borgias."[20] How close is that classroom, in Laforgue's view of it, to
the room in which "the women come and go / Talking of Michel-

18. Laforgue, p. 23.
19. Ibid., p. 36.
20. As translated and cited in Ramsey, *Jules Laforgue*, p. 144.

angelo." All therein is seen as a refraction of the self, including a partial view of the self itself refracted. The feeling one gets in reading much of Laforgue is somewhere between despair and amusement. To laugh at the world's incongruity may also be to laugh at oneself, and only irony can preserve a stable self-possession in such a changing perspective. Is it surprising that Pierrot, that *Commedia* clown and image of gaiety, pathos, and cruelty at once, becomes a focus of roles and perspectives and every poet becomes, in part, an author in search of a character?

If incongruities are at the heart of the Laforguean vision, so are they also for the early poetry of Eliot. But the point here is that Eliot's sense of irony, borne out of the lesson of Laforgue, was both enforced and enriched by his exposure to the thought of F. H. Bradley. Both Laforgue and Bradley are products of the malaise which grew out of the characteristic romantic bifurcation of subject and object; by steeping himself in both, Eliot receives the inheritance in two forms—the poetic and the philosophic. Laforgue's irony and pessimism are an aesthetic counterpart of Bradley's metaphysical paradoxes. Taken together, they present a combined statement of the impasse created by the confusion of subject and object. Eliot's Laforguean poems may precede, chronologically, his concentration on Bradley, but the most representative of those poems, "Prufrock," came at a time when both influences were at work shaping the young Eliot's sensibility. "Prufrock" is both Laforguean and Bradleyan and its larger ironies, however imitative of Laforgue, are also the poetic equivalent of the paradox which, as Eliot had come to see, lay at the heart of Bradley's metaphysic: "All points of view are relative, but all points of view must be sustained." Or, as Eliot himself put it, "Everything, from one point of view, is subjective; and everything, from another point of view, is objective; and there is no *absolute* point of view from which a decision may be pronounced" (*KE*, 21, 22). It is simply the old solipsistic predicament come back to haunt the early twentieth century in its search for an absolute. Eliot is not alone in feeling that it is a central problem of any idealist formulation, nor is he the only writer of his time to reveal, through his work, the subtle and often brilliantly illusory effects of relative perspective.

First Browning, and then Conrad and James, chiefly, had exploited the possibilities of shifting and multiple points of view, and the poems from 1910 to 1922, that is, through *The Waste Land*, all reveal Eliot's debt to those three. It is to James, though, that the predicaments of such "protagonists" as Prufrock and the "lady" of "Portrait" are most closely allied. The Jamesian world of shifting and ambiguous ambiance, of extenuated thought and delicate contemplations, is implicitly behind the quest of Prufrock in his mental journey through the decadent drawing rooms of the mind where people "come and go / Talking of Michelangelo." The lesson from Laforgue makes it possible for Eliot to see the situation ironically and even to mock his persona ("No! I am not Prince Hamlet, nor was meant to be; / Am an attendant lord, one that will do / To swell a progress, start a scene or two"). The preoccupation with point of view, so characteristic of James, provides a key to interpreting the setting of much of Eliot's early poetry, but point of view in those poems comes to be understood in terms of a typical Eliot concern: the failure of communication in a world dominated by the subjective ego. Prufrock's inability to make himself understood by those around him reveals this subjective isolation. The mermaids, whose song suggests some possibility of hope and release, sing only "each to each," and real communication, real confrontation, is more than the subjective self can admit: when "human voices wake us," we "drown." Neither the irony of Laforgue alone nor the solipsism of Bradley would have given Eliot the context in which to envision the problem so that some solution was demanded. One person's failure to communicate himself can be accepted and even overcome, and the quandry over subject–object can be relegated to the remote place of philosophical discourse. But when the subjective self has to function in the midst of a community, or society, and when the dilemma posed by a philosophy like Bradley's is understood to have social consequences, then the failure of language to heal the separation between the self and its surroundings becomes the failure of a society to realize its communal ideals; the intimate, private ironies of the Laforguean persona are evidences of a tragic world peopled with myriads of isolated souls. Prufrock, placed in the context of the city, becomes the "crowd" which "flowed over London Bridge" in *The Waste Land* and which reminded Eliot of the souls of Dante's limbo:

> I had not thought death had undone so many.
> Sighs, short and infrequent, were exhaled,
> And each man fixed his eyes before his feet. (*CP*, 39)

Placed in the social context of *The Waste Land*, language's inability to render meaningful the relationship of one consciousness to another also signals the emptiness of religion and of history. Words are no longer sufficient to reveal absolutes. In "Gerontion," "Signs are taken for wonders," and "The word within a word, [is] unable to speak a word." "Christ the tiger" comes "In depraved May" and the host is only "To be eaten, to be divided, to be drunk / Among whispers." However redemptive such rites may once have been, they are now only memories ironically juxtaposed to Mr. Silvero, Hakagawa, and Madame de Tornquist. Their memory may even be more painful for the realization that time has rendered them inoperative. Since

> History has many cunning passages, contrived corridors
> And issues, deceives with whispering ambitions,
> Guides us by vanities. (*CP*, 22)

memory may serve simply to reinforce our own sense of being beyond the reach of grace or forgiveness.

Similarly, in *The Waste Land*, faith and action are felt as possible only in a past, and the poem's allusiveness is thus more than merely a technical device. On the landscape of the mind capable of thinking only its own reflected image, it is impossible to locate "The roots that clutch," the "branches [that] grow." The materials of a hopeful vision cannot be given coherence until something external to the self removes the "Shadow" falling "Between the idea / And the reality / Between the motion / And the act" ("The Hollow Men," *CP*, 58). Words must be released from their subjective participation in the life of the ego before any potentially religious language can become the vehicle of faith. Language conceived in the categories of an idealist epistemology cannot be made to serve the demands of a faith grounded in the revelation of Absolute Being.

So the paradox in Bradley ("Everything, from one point of view, is subjective; and everything, from another point of view, is objective; and there is no *absolute* point of view from which a decision may be pronounced") and the private ironies of Laforgue, when treated within the larger context of society, reveal a characteristic emptiness of modern life and point to that failure of the self to reach out to others so typical of the sense of alienation found in the writers of the early part of this century. This part of the romantic inheritance Eliot shared with his contemporary Pound he may well have learned from his reading of James. Certainly James contributed to his growing awareness, in the early part of his career, of the consequences of subjectivism when placed in a broad social and cultural context: "His [James'] romanticism implied no defect in observation of the things he wanted to observe; it was not the romanticism of those who dream because they are too lazy or too fearful to face the fact; it issues, rather, from the imperative insistence of an ideal which tormented him. He was possessed by the vision of an ideal society; he *saw* (not fancied) the relations between the members of such a society. And no one, in the end, had ever been more aware—or with more benignity, or less bitterness—of the disparity between possibility and fact."[21] Prufrock's dilemma results from the disparity between possibility and fact, but as we have already noted, that dilemma is figured forth in terms of the persona's failure to communicate. *The Waste Land* also treats man in his dilemma between possibility and fact, but the context of the poem is expanded to include the whole of a people, with London standing for a race at a particular juncture in time and place. It is, after all, a longer poem than any Eliot had previously written, a sort of poetic *novella* with a number of perplexed and stultified characters.

That the disparity between possibility and fact was early seen by Eliot to be a disparity between word and deed is chiefly a result of the lessons of Laforgue and Bradley. But had he never sensed the social consequences of that disparity, he might have gone on multiplying Prufrocks and never arrived at the historical and cultural complexity which we rightly associate with the Eliot of *The Waste Land* and after. To discover a way, through language, of bridging the gap (itself revealed in language) between word and deed, between possibility and fact, is the central concern of all the poetry subsequent to *The Waste Land*. The necessity of the struggle is nowhere more clearly revealed to Eliot than in his early efforts to be the public critic, to be able to say something about the role of the poet and the function of his product which can have broad, even

21. "A Prediction in Regard to Three English Authors," *Vanity Fair*, 21 (February, 1924): 29. The critical debt of Eliot to James is treated at some length by Alan Holder in "T. S. Eliot on Henry James," *PMLA*, 79 (September, 1964): 490–97.

universal, significance for a public audience. If the gradually expanding social context of the poetry from "Prufrock" through *The Waste Land* served to bring home to Eliot the far-reaching consequences of idealistic stalemate and private irony, the early ventures into the realm of literary and cultural criticism made it evident to him that something beyond the self-enclosed ego must be located and fixed in language if either the poetry or the criticism were to have permanent meaning. Prufrock, alone in the drawing rooms of his mind, is pathetically ironic, but Prufrock multiplied into the crowds flowing over London Bridge is an emblem of the romantic tragedy and the consequent dehumanization of the world.

2
The Critical Lesson

So this is this, and that is that:
And that's how you AD-DRESS A CAT.

Writing in 1933, in *The Use of Poetry and the Use of Criticism,* Eliot said of his role as critic: "I have no general theory of my own. . . . The extreme of theorising about the nature of poetry, the essence of poetry if there is any, belongs to the study of aesthetics and is no concern of the poet or of a critic with my limited qualifications."[1] The tone is familiar and the disclaimer characteristic. It is of a piece with his concern to be thought of as a poet who incidentally practices criticism rather than a critic who from time to time writes poems. Though, like all pertinent literary criticism, it is empirical and after the fact, its variations and contradictions are the result of a growing, changing mind rather than the lack of any consistent attitudes toward aesthetic matters. Behind every critical statement, however slight, there is a metaphysical view, though the critic himself may be happily unaware of its shape. Criticism reflects a world just as much as poetry does, though admittedly with more room for digression and less need for concision.

The world of Eliot's criticism has, to be sure, never been noted as having the kind of aesthetic or philosophical or theological direction of, say, the criticism of Coleridge or Arnold, to both of whom Eliot is indebted in a number of ways. But it is true that Eliot's writing about poetry and literary matters in general describes a pattern not unlike that which marks his growth and change as poet and dramatist. Moreover, some of the problems pointed up by his early poetry are directly attacked, from a different point of view, in his first critical ventures. There is throughout his career, then, a kind of dialectic between his critical voice and his practice as a poet and, one adjusting and modifying the other, both of them move toward a single end.[2]

1. Pp. 143, 149–50.
2. The possibility of interpreting Eliot's criticism itself as a constant interchange of opposites has been explored at length, but with little result of any

As I have already suggested, the voice of the personae in the poems in *Prufrock and Other Observations* and the Laforguean imitations in the *Poems* of 1919 is that of the isolated and entrapped self, caught in a world of utter subjectivity and unable to effect any communication beyond its own isolation. Through 1919, the small utterance of the pathetic Prufrock is dominant in Eliot's poetry. The first major criticism appears in collected form just after that time with the publication in 1920 of *The Sacred Wood*. The essays there can be viewed, in part, as Eliot's first attempt to use criticism as a means of trying a solution to some of the problems raised by the poetry which immediately precedes it. There are two kinds of essay in that first collection and they will be the kinds which will dominate all the rest of Eliot's critical writing. They demand close examination for that reason, and also because they represent his earliest attempt to use criticism to advance his own thinking about the nature of poetry and, hence, of language.

The first kind of criticism, of which Eliot was to write very little, we might call the historically general; "Tradition and the Individual Talent" is certainly one of his most important examples of this.[3] The Prufrockian trap might be overcome if, by chance, history itself could be viewed as a larger mind within which the mind of each individual poet could take its place. The "individual talent" when admired for its own individuality produces the conditions which mark the extremities of Romanticism, and the poet comes close to being regarded as a prophet of revelation, or even a priest of a new faith. This in turn leads to an impasse, and what began as freedom from past convention and restraint finally develops into a horrible ego-involvement driving one to wander aimlessly, like Prufrock, in the rooms of his own mind. Language freed from all past conventions becomes private and the poet who uses language thus can speak only to himself. So Eliot censures the later Blake because what "his genius required, and what it sadly lacked, was a framework of accepted and traditional ideas which would have prevented him from indulging in a philosophy of his own . . ."(*SW*, 157–58).

---

value, by Fei-Pai Lu, *T. S. Eliot, The Dialectical Structure of His Theory of Poetry* (Chicago, 1966).

3. Robert Penn Warren speaks of it as being "in many ways the germinal essay of Eliot's whole thought, specifically of his literary thought." See "Eliot's Literary Criticism," in *T. S. Eliot: The Man and His Work*, ed. Allen Tate (New York, 1966), p. 282.

Tradition, that is, to Eliot, a particularly specifiable body of literary practice, generally Latin in its origins and bound more or less by common understandings of the nature of the world, is needed to modify the egocentrism of the "individual talent": "No poet, no artist of any art, has his complete meaning alone. His significance, his appreciation is the appreciation of his relation to the dead poets and artists" (SW, 49). And this dictum is for Eliot "a principle of aesthetic, not merely historical, criticism" (SW, 49). Eliot's insistence on this as a matter of aesthetic criticism is important, for it reveals again how clearly he is indebted in his early work to Bradley. Eliot's assumption of a universal artistic attitude, having its own criteria and direction and existing apart from other attitudes (such as the historical), is closely related to Bradley's conception of a universal subconscious, now and again expressed in the production of individual finite centers. Individuals are known, thereby, not merely through their uniqueness, but also through the degree in which they share in the Absolute, or pervasive Finite Center. Too much emphasis upon the uniqueness of one's own personality can prevent the artist from recognizing the order and unity provided by the larger "personality" of tradition. For Eliot, this larger "personality" is composed of the "dead poets and artists," and it partakes in turn of the still larger entity which he calls "the mind of Europe." That "mind" is what the poet "learns in time to be much more important than his own private mind" (SW, 51).

The first portion of "Tradition and the Individual Talent" is devoted to developing the character of that mind, how the poet can know it and how he can best relate to it. In the first place, it is not something which improves, or progresses in any evolutionary fashion. Yet it changes, "and . . . this change is a development which abandons nothing *en route*, which does not superannuate either Shakespeare, or Homer, or the rock drawing of the Magdalenian draughtsmen" (SW, 51). The change may be a "refinement perhaps," a "complication certainly," but in no sense, from the "point of view of the artist, any improvement" (SW, 51).

It is therefore incumbent upon the poet that he have an awareness of the *presentness* of the past, rather than an interest in the past for any antiquarian reasons. And the way he may acquire that awareness is through noting how his own work, once done, becomes a part of it and thus alters it ever so slightly. He has to give himself over, as it were, to that mind which precedes him and gives meaning to his effort, which without it might not be possible. "What happens," Eliot says, "is a continual surrender of [the poet] as he is at the moment to something which is more valuable. The progress of an artist is a continual self-sacrifice, a continual extinction of personality" (SW, 52–53).

Much has been said about the place this doctrine of impersonality plays in the work of Eliot, and it is even brought up from time to time to explain the particular lack of individual intensity some readers find in such late works as the *Quartets*. But it should be kept in mind that the formulation of this notion comes early in the poet's career, and before many years pass it will undergo some important modifications. In part (it is easy to see this now) Eliot was simply reacting against the cult of personality which characterized much of the poetry and criticism of the late nineteenth century, from Wilde's inversion of art and life to the proliferation of Browning Societies in England and America. So far as this is true, crying down the personality of the poet is but a logical response to the predicament of Prufrock, benumbed by too much personality. But it is more than a reaction to something existing in the literature of a previous time; it is a reaction to something to which Eliot's own early speculations and poetic experience had led him. It is an attempt to modify his sensibility and to modify it in such a way as to make further poetry possible. The cult of personality produces novelty and while "novelty is better than repetition . . . tradition is a matter of much wider significance." It cannot be inherited, and "it involves . . . the historical sense, which we may call nearly indispensable to anyone who would continue to be a poet beyond his twenty-fifth year . . ." (SW, 49). Thus, tradition and the "historical sense" provide a larger context for confession and self-expression, and the mind of the individual poet is made a part of the more enduring mind of his literary past which, in this case, is the mind of Europe.

But the essential materials which poetry has to transmit are emotions and feelings. Though the "effect of a work of art upon the person who enjoys it is an experience different in kind from any experience not of art," the effect must be formed out of emotions: "It may be formed out of one emotion, or may be a combination of several . . ." (SW, 54). However it may form itself, emotion and feeling are its constituents and an insistence upon this runs throughout "Tradition and the Individual Talent" and indeed all the essays in *The Sacred Wood*. How then can the poet who has sacrificed his personality to the large entity called "the mind of Europe" convey any meaningful emotion or feeling?

Eliot's answer reveals the extent to which he is still caught by the limitation of variable points of view: "Just as idealism and materialism are both equally true and false, according to one's point of view, so each mind is a private world and at the same time a perspective on a social world which it interpenetrates."[4] The emotion of the private mind may be suspect, but it can be transformed when the poet partakes of the best which has been collected from the emotive store of the race and preserved by tradition. The peculiar and proper task of any new poet is to refine his own emotions in the light of tradition and to use the materials which his tradition provides him to arrange his personal experience in new ways. The personal experience of the new poet interacts with the experiences of the "dead poets and artists" and in the process is refined and ordered to produce new works which are, at the same time, additions to the accumulations of tradition.

This idea of interaction leads Eliot to compare the poet to a chemical catalyst: "The mind of the poet is the shred of platinum," which, placed with two inert gases, causes them to react to form a new combination. The platinum remains "inert, neutral, and unchanged. . . . The mind of the poet may partly or exclusively operate upon the experience of the man himself; but, the more perfect the artist, the more completely separate in him will be the man who suffers and the mind which creates . . ." (SW, 54). Eliot is, of course, not saying that the poet does not experience, or suffer, but rather that he must not write solely out of his private suffering. He must learn to disguise his subjective experience in the garb of others' experiences; that is, he must be responsive to the ways which have been traditionally established for expressing personal experience and use those ways to give his own experience universal meaning. In other words, the good poet writes his own experiences in the light of the ways his predecessors have written theirs. "The poet's mind is in fact a receptacle for seizing and storing up numberless feelings, phrases, images, which remain there until all the particles which can unite to form a new compound are present together" (SW, 55). Eliot recognized the difficulty of such a notion and sensed something almost mystical about it. He relates it, at

4. Miller, *Poets*, p. 156.

one point, to "the metaphysical theory of the substantial unity of the soul; for my meaning is, that the poet has, not a 'personality' to express, but a particular medium, which is only a medium and not a personality, in which impressions and experiences combine in peculiar and unexpected ways" (SW, 56). But here the emphasis is perhaps misleading, for as we have seen, Eliot recognizes the fact that the poet, however much he may translate his subjective experience into an impersonal "medium," is always working from that experience.

The mind of Europe, the poet as catalyst, the poet as medium— all these notions have something in common, namely, that there is an already existing unity to the world of emotion, feeling, and image which the artist must learn to assimilate and put into new config- urations. Taken together, these ideas add up to a revision and re- statement of Coleridge's concept of organic unity. But Eliot, unlike Coleridge, insists it is necessary for the poet to subjugate his own subjective ego to the larger mental space which precedes his own and makes his own possible. The appeal of tradition, therefore, does not really solve the Prufrockian dilemma, for understanding himself as part of the "mind of Europe" only enlarges the poet's point of view; it does not remove its subjectivity, for point of view remains the factor determining whether the poet will write good or ill. Any escape from one's private personality into the reaches of the mind of tradition is but a substitution of a larger for a smaller world of experience. However much Eliot would want to deny the poet's personality ("only those who have personality and emotions know what it means to escape from these things" [SW, 58]), in the final analysis, he cannot do it. After all, it is one's personality which determines his taste, and taste, rather than any objective criteria, must be the relevant feature in the makeup of the poet who as- pires to write new and not just novel poetry.[5]

Perhaps sensing that his attempt to define the creative role of the poet has led him into vague and difficult regions, Eliot proclaims, in

5. The role taste plays in shaping Eliot's idea of poetry is perhaps not so evident as in forming his concepts of society as a whole. Though it is not within the scope of this study, much might be learned about the influence Eliot had in the thirties on the ideas of the Southern Agrarians by exploring his idea of heredity and cultural refinement as it is expressed in *Notes Toward the Definition of Culture* (New York, 1949). Proper authority in the social and political realms is often there made a matter of the special sensibility of a cul- tivated elite, i.e., a matter of aristocratic taste.

the second part of "Tradition and the Individual Talent," that the best use of criticism is to divert "interest from the poet to the poetry . . . for it would conduce to a juster estimation of actual poetry, good or bad" (SW, 59). The shift is instructive, for it points up the inherent failure of the concept of a universal mind to replace satisfactorily the more limited individual ego of the subjective self, as represented by a Prufrock. Since Eliot's "impersonal theory of poetry merely substitutes a universal mind for a private one,"[6] the poet is left where he began—with a world entirely made up of mind and unyielding to concrete statement because of its subjective existence. Eliot himself is aware of the difficulty, and he ends his theoretical speculation in "Tradition and the Individual Talent" by saying that this "essay proposes to halt at the frontier of metaphysics or mysticism, and confine itself to such practical conclusions as can be applied by the responsible person interested in poetry" (SW, 59). Thus he points to the other kind of essay which constitutes the remainder of *The Sacred Wood,* namely, exercises in practical criticism.

But what of language itself, and its place in criticism and poetry? The reader of "Tradition and the Individual Talent" is likely to be struck by the manner in which Eliot seems to take language for granted. Poetry is constructed of "feelings, phrases, images." Words and feelings and emotions appear to be interchangeable, hence identical. One is almost tempted to say that Eliot, at least in this essay, is unaware that poetry is made up of words at all. And that is just the point: the problem of language for the early Eliot is not a dualistic one. Subject and object are not pitted against one another, any more for the poet than for his personae. Since the world is all subject, and subject to the thinking mind, then language itself is there, formed and tried by past use and practice. The poet's task is to find the best way to put it into new patterns which will express his own time and place and yet reveal his sense of the past. Prufrock's problem is not the result of living in a world where things have no names, but of his inability to order those names so that the resulting phrases and images will point beyond himself.

His world is fragmented ("I should have been a pair of ragged claws / Scuttling across the floors of silent seas"), but the fragments all have names, at least to his own cognition. Again, we can see a reason for Eliot's appeal to a proper "historical sense." If the larger

6. Miller, *Poets,* p. 159.

mind of the past does indeed exist, then it exists partly as the trans-
mitter of a massive language which for all its variety is in fact one.
Languages vary, but language is universal, for it is what makes the
continuity of tradition both real and possible. Moreover, for the
poet who fully grasps this fact, language is no longer merely his
own, limited by his particular time and place, but contains the
wealth of all the people who have preceded him and who have had
feelings, experiences, emotions similar to his own. Language is both
a vehicle of tradition *and* a traditional vehicle, and the poet can
avail himself of it to the degree to which he can divest himself of
his own ego, his own personality. But the problem remains, though
the rhetoric of "Tradition and the Individual Talent" tends to obscure it: in what way is a larger subjectivity better than a smaller
one?

Though the essays which follow in *The Sacred Wood* do not in
themselves provide either an answer or a solution, they do suggest
some of the directions in which Eliot was gradually to move in
finding a way out of the dilemma. First, the attention that is given
to particular poems and particular poets is suggestive, for while
the speculation of the seminal essay in the collection remains vague
and disturbing, the criticism in the following essays is at least specific
and continually rounding on an object made of words. Even the
titles of several of them reflect this practical tendency ("The Possibility of a Poetic Drama," " 'Rhetoric' and Poetic Drama," "Notes on
the Blank Verse of Christopher Marlowe," "Swinburne as Poet").
While they certainly do not contain any radical departure from the
"programme for the *metier* of poetry" (*SE*, 52), set down in "Tradition and the Individual Talent," they do provide the basis for
some new discoveries and, perhaps as exercises, served to reveal to
their writer some possible ways leading out of the problem of
subjectivity.

The most explicit remarks about language in *The Sacred Wood*
are to be found in " 'Rhetoric' and Poetic Drama" and "Notes on the
Blank Verse of Christopher Marlowe." In the former there is some
hint of how in drama that "precise statement of life which is at the
same time a point of view" can be achieved. Though "no conversational or other form . . . can be applied indiscriminately . . . if a
writer wishes to give the effect of speech he must positively give
the effect of himself talking in his own person or in one of his roles."
More importantly, "If we are to express ourselves, our variety of

thoughts and feelings, on a variety of subjects with inevitable rightness, we must adapt our manner to the moment with infinite variations" (SW, 80). Such variety of expression was a chief characteristic of the Elizabethan playwrights: "Examination of the development of Elizabethan drama shows this progress in adaptation, a development from monotony to variety, a progressive elaboration of the means of expressing these variations. This drama is admitted to have grown away from the rhetorical expression, the bombast speeches, of Kyd and Marlowe to the subtle and dispersed utterance of Shakespeare and Webster. But this apparent abandonment or outgrowth of rhetoric is two things; *it is partly an improvement in language and it is partly progressive variation in feeling*" (SW, 80, italics mine). Feeling and language which expresses feeling are still considered as nearly the same thing, but the phrasing here places a distinction upon language itself which is new to Eliot's remarks on this matter. As feeling becomes more subtle, more varied, language itself may undergo some improvement, and the implication is that such improvement is marked by a trend away from convention ("the rhetorical expression, the bombast speeches") toward a more natural speech, or at least toward language akin to that used in daily converse. Articulateness comes to be identified with clarity of communication: valid emotions can only be known as such when clearly expressed. "Some writers appear to believe that emotions gain in intensity through being inarticulate. Perhaps the emotions are not significant enough to endure full daylight" (SW, 84).

This emerging distinction between emotion and language, not as yet fully realized, has been generally overlooked by commentators on the early Eliot. As Eliot gradually makes it sharper, he also treats aspects of language which play importantly in his major plays and later poetry. In time, he views language as the vehicle of design and pattern, not so much through the ideas it conveys as through the natural rhythms it evokes. Prufrock's dilemma may in time be overcome not by the naming of new objects, but by the careful attention to certain patterns of existence which are mirrored in the natural patterns of speech and song.

There is even clearer indication Eliot is thinking in this direction in "Notes on the Blank Verse of Christopher Marlowe" when he says that the "verse accomplishments of *Tamburlaine* are notably two: Marlowe gets into blank verse the melody of Spenser, and he gets a new driving power by reinforcing the sentence period against the line period" (SW, 91). The chief dramatic value of the "verse accomplishments" is that they enhance meaning not by explicit statement or by rhetorical convention, but by setting up melodic patterns which reach beyond the immediate reference of the words themselves. Eliot remarks, in "Ben Jonson," that if one examines "the first hundred lines or more of *Volpone* the verse . . . looks like mere 'rhetoric,' certainly not 'deeds and language such as men do use'!" But it is not "mere rhetoric," because it is maintained consistently throughout and thus "conveys in the end an effect not of verbosity, but of bold, even shocking and terrifying directness" (SW, 114). Granted, this is not altogether clear, but one can fairly assume that for Eliot the thing which keeps Jonson's "rhetoric" from being only that is its being employed in an extended pattern; since that is all there is, it takes on the aspect of naturalness, does not stand out from a texture of a different kind. Again, what Eliot seems to be approving is pattern, even simple repetition.

In the essay "Philip Massinger" we get a further hint as to what might constitute an improvement of language. Certain lines of Tourneur and Middleton, Eliot says, "exhibit that perpetual slight alteration of language, words perpetually juxtaposed in new and sudden combinations, meanings perpetually *eingeschachtelt* into meanings . . . which evidences . . . a development of the English language which we have perhaps never equalled" (SW, 129). This suggestion leads Eliot to another, later to be developed in the famous essay on the metaphysical poets, that the seventeenth century represented a period when "the intellect was immediately at the tips of the senses." At that time "sensation became word and word was sensation" (SW, 129).

In the essay following, Eliot makes the fullest statement of what can be clearly seen now as a developing awareness that words may possibly be made to reach beyond their immediate, subjective, and denotative ends when arranged into some patterns almost but not quite the same as musical notes. In this regard, the nice distinctions among verse, poetry, and music are important: ". . . in any case the beauty or effect of sound is neither that of music nor that of poetry which can be set to music. There is no reason why verse intended to be sung should not present a sharp visual image or convey an important intellectual meaning, for it supplements the music by another means of affecting the feelings. What we get in Swinburne is an expression by sound, which could not possibly associate itself with music. For what he gives is not images and ideas and music, it is one thing with a curious mixture of suggestions of all three" (SW, 146).

How is this mixture effected in the poetry of Swinburne? On this point, Eliot fails to be precise—because words fail him, since the thing he is trying to pin down is itself beyond the realm of words, at least in their denotative use. He comes closest to explanation when he praises Swinburne for achieving a union of word and object to such a degree that the two are for all intents and purposes one and the same. In other words, Swinburne succeeds because he renders a world of unity, and his use of language denies the typical Romantic duality of subject and object, word and thing: "Language in a healthy state presents the object, is so close to the object that the two are identified" (SW, 149). In Swinburne's poetry the two are identified "because the object has ceased to exist, because the meaning is merely the hallucination of meaning, because language, uprooted, has adapted itself to an independent life of atmospheric nourishment" (SW, 149).

Without saying so directly, Eliot seems to have sensed that in Swinburne, as in certain of the Elizabethan dramatists, patterns of sound, analogous to those of speech but heightened and sustained, approaching something akin to musical forms, have so supplemented the mere word that the result is a blending of subject and object and exists in its own right outside of and beyond the subjectivity of the mind. The ability to achieve this union of word and object, of word and deed, becomes a criterion of the goodness or badness of a poet: "The bad poet dwells partly in a world of objects and partly in a world of words, and he never can get them to fit" (SW, 150). Prufrock is, in that sense, a bad poet, and the condition he represents is indicative of the larger condition discussed earlier. But transferring the individual mind to some larger entity, say, "the mind of Europe," does not of itself solve the problem, for that too is but a manifestation of point of view, of the individual's subjectivity. The compass of discourse may be enlarged, but how can one be sure of communicating with anything beyond an expanded pantheon of the dead poets and artists? Suggestions of an answer can be seen in those essays in practical criticism which form the bulk of The Sacred Wood. Their very method (comparison and contrast) implies a dialogue, someone speaking to someone else. Again and again, Eliot juxtaposes the lines of one poet to those of another and lets one comment upon the other. Increasingly, there is a sense that the level of communication involves more than the denotative meanings of the words themselves. Somes lines *sound* better than others, some patterns are more compelling than others. The music of verse (and music implies pattern) begins to take on more and more importance, partly because Eliot seems to feel that it may express those things which are, in some sense, inexpressible.

Even so brief a survey as this of the major essays in *The Sacred Wood* points up two things: one, Eliot's attempt (in "Tradition and the Individual Talent") to expand the individual consciousness into a larger, traditional, and even universal consciousness and, more significantly, his initial explorations in a practical criticism. It is through the latter, less speculative exercise that he came gradually to form what was to become in time his most important conception of what poetry is and how it functions. However much "Tradition and the Individual Talent" lays the groundwork for Eliot's subsequent criticism, it is clear that such a program as he outlined there has severe limitations. If the main lines of thought pursued in "Tradition" are later fruitful of further speculation, such developments are best looked for in the essays in social and political critique, such as *Notes Towards the Definition of Culture* and *The Idea of a Christian Society*. The literary criticism Eliot wrote after *The Sacred Wood* moved continually in the direction of modifications in the program found in "Tradition." His own experience of other poetry, particularly the work of the Elizabethan dramatists and of Dante, served to adjust the rigidity of his concept of the depersonalization of poetry and its attendant idea of a collective mind. History itself may decide, especially when it is viewed from within the confines of the self-enclosed ego. "Think now," says the speaker in "Gerontion,"

> History has many cunning passages, contrived corridors
> And issues, deceives with whispering ambitions,
> Guides us by vanities. (*CP*, 22)

There is, after *The Sacred Wood*, an increased critical attention given to the role sound and rhythmic pattern play in establishing meaning in poetry. In 1933, in lectures given at Harvard while he was Charles Eliot Norton Professor of Poetry and subsequently published as *The Use of Poetry and the Use of Criticism*, Eliot was to use a phrase to cover this aspect of the poet's art which was later to have wide currency. In his lecture on Matthew Arnold, Eliot announced that what the poet chiefly lacked was the "auditory imagination," and he went on to define that as "the feeling for syllable and rhythm, penetrating far below the conscious levels of thought and feeling, invigorating every word; sinking to the most primitive and forgotten, returning to the origin and bringing something back, seeking the beginning and the end. It works through meanings, certainly, or not without meanings in the ordinary sense, and fuses the old and obliterated and the trite, the current, and the new and surprising, the most ancient and the most civilized mentality" (*UPC*, 118–19). Shakespeare excels all other English poets because he had such an imagination, whereas, for all their merit, Pope and Dryden did not. Arnold did, however, have taste ("to be able to quote as Arnold could is the best evidence of taste"); that is, he had a proper understanding of the past and its relevance to the present. In short, he had the requisite historical sense demanded by Eliot in "Tradition and the Individual Talent." But although in that essay the possession of a right historical sense, coupled with the ability to sacrifice personality on the part of the poet, would have seemed sufficient to make a poet good, there is evident here a necessary third criterion. We can go even further and say that by 1933, Eliot was less concerned with the historical sense (perhaps recognizing its latent subjectivity) and largely occupied with defining the goodness of poetry in terms of its musical properties.

Much later, in "The Music of Poetry" (1942), Eliot further amplifies the concept of the "auditory imagination." English verse is particularly rich in examples of imagination since, in part, it has taken so much from other languages. It may even be possible, Eliot suggests, "that the beauty of some English poetry is due to the presence of more than one metrical structure in it. . . . What I think we have . . . is a kind of amalgam of systems of divers sources . . . an amalgam like the amalgam of races, and indeed partly due to racial origins" (*OP*, 20). Here we have the older concept of a universal consciousness, or even the notion of "the mind of Europe" under a new guise and serving a new end. "The rhythms of Anglo-Saxon, Celtic, Norman French, of Middle English and Scots, have all made their mark upon English poetry, together with the rhythms of Latin, and, at various periods, of French, Italian and Spanish." But one principle underlies the degree of effectiveness which may in any case result from this mixture: "the law that poetry must not stray too far from the ordinary everyday language which we use and hear. Whether poetry is accentual or syllabic, rhymed, or rhymeless, formal or free, it cannot afford to lose its contact with the changing language of common intercourse" (*OP*, 20–21).

Sound must not be considered as something apart from sense: "the music of poetry is not something which exists apart from the meaning" (*OP*, 21). But where sound and sense divide is not easily determined. The degree to which a poem moves us (touches our emotions?) may be a measure of its validity as poetry, even though we may not understand the language. On the other hand, understanding the language is no guarantee that the poem will move us as poetry. There is an area where, in effect, words do not go and it is there that the combination of meaning and sound has to take over: "the poet is occupied with frontiers of consciousness beyond which words fail, though meanings still exist . . . ambiguities may be due to the fact that the poem means more, not less, than ordinary speech can communicate" (*OP*, 22–23). These are curious utterances for anyone concerned with making words convey *particular* meanings, and such remarks as these have done much to bring about a contemporary reaction to Eliot as a poet who essentially resisted the very mode in which he was committed to work.[7] But given a condition wherein language itself cannot be held to exist apart from point of view, wherein words in their denotative value point exasperatingly back to their speaker, it is not surprising that some effort might be made to explore the possibility that language, used in certain ways, might point beyond itself.

About the time of his work on *The Waste Land*, Eliot's attentiveness to ritual and myth is of a piece with his growing awareness that language itself may reveal meanings through patterns which approach music, but which are for the most part neither overt nor explicit. Patterns in language may themselves become ritual patterns or designs which work upon the mind in ways which are difficult to define. Eliot thinks that this takes place in certain Elizabethan plays.

In his 1934 essay on John Marston, he speaks of something in *Sophonisba* which cannot be directly described, but which shapes

7. One of the most illuminating appraisals of Eliot's conception of the "auditory imagination" is Helen Gardner's in *The Art of T. S. Eliot* (New York, 1959), pp. 3–35.

one's response to the play just as surely as the drama's most overt actions and speeches: "a pattern behind the pattern into which the characters deliberately involve themselves; the kind of pattern . . . we perceive only at rare moments of inattention and detachment, drowsing in sunlight" (*SE*, 232). Here, of course, the pattern is essentially a dramatic one, involving action and movement, and not just one of words alone. But the quotations Eliot uses to introduce this observation make it clear that one place where such patterns manifest themselves is the language which shapes and gives meaning to those actions and movements.[8] And it is worth noting that this appears to take place in moments of inattention and detachment, when in fact the mind is not closely attentive to overt meanings, but is perhaps rather responding to some sort of repetition, even incantation, which the language of the play sets up. In one sense, all drama is ritual, and ritual has a particular linguistic dimension, just as language can be understood to have a particular ritualistic aspect.

In Eliot's view, recognition of this relationship is one of the reasons for Dante's greatness. In his major essay on Dante, in 1929, he introduces a corollary to his notion of the "auditory imagination." Dante possessed a "visual imagination . . . in the sense that he lived in an age in which men still saw visions. It was a psycho-

8. Eliot cites a number of passages from *Sophonisba* to make his point, but the most significant is a portion from the scene in which the witch Erictho takes on the form of Sophonisba in order to induce Syphax to lie with her. Eliot remarks that this is not merely a scene of "Gratuitous horror, introduced . . . to make our flesh creep; it is integral to the plot of the play; and is one of those moments of a double reality, in which Marston is saying something else . . ." (*SE*, 230). To support this contention, Eliot cites the following passage from the scene, a passage which bears striking similarity to a number from *Murder in the Cathedral*:

> though Heaven bears
> A face far from us, gods have most long ears;
> Jove has a hundred marble hands.
> Nothing in Nature is unserviceable,
> No, not even inutility itself.
> Is then for nought dishonesty in being?
> And if it be sometimes of forced use,
> Wherein more urgent than in saving nations?
>
> Our vows, our faith, our oaths, why they're ourselves.
>
> Gods naught forsee, but see, for to their eyes
> Naught is to come or past; nor are you vile
> Because the gods forsee; for gods, not we
> See as things are; things are not as we see
> (as cited in *SE*, 231).

logical habit, the trick of which we have forgotten. . . . We have nothing but dreams, and we have forgotten that seeing visions—a practice now relegated to the aberrant and uneducated—was once a more significant, interesting, and disciplined kind of dreaming" (SE, 243). But the "visual imagination" of Dante would never have been able to express itself had he not understood the need for a simple language, one which makes its impression on the mind of the reader partly through repetition and reiteration.[9] A style such as Dante's reveals that "the greatest poetry can be written with the greatest economy of words, and with the greatest austerity in the use of metaphor, simile, verbal beauty, and elegance" (SE, 252). This bareness, this simplicity which Eliot associates with Dante is also a feature of a common language, a language close to the primitive sources (in the historical sense) of the emotions of a people: "The language of each great English poet is his own language; the language of Dante is the perfection of a common language" (SE, 252). That this was so is partly the result of fortunate historical circumstance, for "the Italian vernacular of the late Middle Ages was still very close to Latin," since the men who used it, like Dante, "were trained, in philosophy and all abstract subjects, in mediaeval Latin" (SE, 239).

But, by contrast, modern languages tend to represent divisions and differences, both racial and national ("When you read modern philosophy, in English, French, German, and Italian, you must be struck by national or racial differences of thought"), which in turn point to even more debilitating divisions: "modern languages *tend* to separate abstract thought (mathematics is the only universal language)" while "mediaeval Latin tended to concentrate on what men of various races and languages could think together" (SE, 239). Dante therefore benefits, in his own language, by the close connection Italian had with Medieval Latin, for it "seems if anything to emphasize . . . universality, because it cuts across the modern division of nationality. . . . Dante, none the less an Italian and a patriot, is first a European" (SE, 239).

Dante combines the two, an appropriate "visual imagination" and a necessary "auditory imagination," to such a degree that his poetry

9. That Dante's use of language is complex and varied, anything but simple, is evident. But what is important here is not the fact of Dante's linguistic variety but the way Eliot understood Dante's practice. For a penetrating discussion of this point, see Mario Praz, "T. S. Eliot as Critic," in *T. S. Eliot: The Man and His Work*, pp. 273–76.

is easy to read and has "a peculiar lucidity—a *poetic* as distinguished from an *intellectual* lucidity. The thought may be obscure, but the word is lucid, or rather translucent" (*SE*, 239). Thus, if language can be made "translucent," patterns which lie behind the words themselves can be revealed, patterns which reach beyond any poet's particular time and place. Only in this fashion can the larger patterns of experience be revealed, can the limited and futilely trapped self find a way which points beyond its own subjectivity. To know that "la sua voluntate e nostra pace" is to know first of all that there is design which overrides our daily comings and goings, and then to be able to place oneself within the context of that larger pattern not of our making. Such is the direction in which Eliot's criticism points, though in oblique and not always consistent ways.

So the critical experience that begins with "Tradition and the Individual Talent" moves to modify the program set forth there. He discovers that the enlargement of the individual consciousness to include all of past literary endeavor, to embrace "the mind of Europe," is not sufficient to overcome the limitation of a private point of view; by turning toward the practical examination of other works from other times, Eliot incorporates a realization that language must be approached from perspectives other than the purely historical. Indeed, language may embody patterns not bound to the denotative meaning of individual words or phrases, and can be used to make certain of those patterns (analogous to basic human emotions) available for the poetic performance.

But the importance of the collective personality, so insisted upon in "Tradition and the Individual Talent," cannot be dismissed. All past literature forms a living whole, and the poet must be conscious of this and work to adjust himself to it. Nothing which he introduces into his poetry can justifiably come from without the existing mind of Europe and so his work must therefore be, as Miller says, to "rearrange and synthesize images, motifs, phrases which are inherited from the past."[10] The growing emphasis upon language as a vehicle of cultural and emotional patterns which exist *outside* the poet is not a radical departure from anything said in "Tradition" but rather a modification of it and an exploration of how that essay's program can be implemented. The assumption that the poet can encompass the collective consciousness begins to show itself

10. *Poets*, p. 172.

as early as *The Waste Land*, where the reader is immediately placed within the mind of all the voices in the poem, both those past and those present. But there, as in "Gerontion," the method is largely an allusive one, and the need for the finely tuned "auditory imagination" has not yet shown itself in Eliot's poetry.

In these poems, the mind of Europe has been made a part of the subjective view of the speaker of the poem. The language of these two poems does not point beyond itself for there is nothing there to point beyond; it is enigmatic. But with "Ash Wednesday" a change is evident, and it is not merely a change in subject. That poem and those to follow reveal an increasing sensitivity to the power of repetition, of incantatory verse, of verbal patterning, and this sensitivity is nowhere more acute than in the early plays, especially in *Murder in the Cathedral*.

The early plays, like the early criticism, provide a ground for experimentation, and the lessons learned there will move nearer to that place where "Every phrase and every sentence is an end and a beginning, / Every poem an epitaph" ("Little Gidding," *CP*, 144). But that cannot be effected without the experiment of the early plays and the poetry of the thirties, without the trying "to learn to use words. . . ."

3

The Thirties

Experiment in Poetry and Drama

> *Why should I Mourn*
> *The vanished power of the*
> *usual reign?*

ELIOT'S WORK in the thirties cannot be approached from any vantage point more revealing than that offered by *The Waste Land*. By now, this poem has taken its place alongside a small number of poems in English which are rightly spoken of as major, in and of themselves. It has been attacked, revered, imitated, even despised, but it remains and probably will remain for generations to come one of the literary watersheds of the twentieth century. Like Picasso's "Guernica," it is one of the testaments of the artistic temper of what we consider the modern era and, thereby, one of the media by which we have come to know ourselves as living in that time.

Yet the distance between the method of *The Waste Land* and that of Eliot's preceding poems seemed so great in 1931 that Edmund Wilson could say that *"The Waste Land*, in method as well as in mood, has left Laforgue far behind. Eliot has developed a new technique, at once laconic, quick and precise, for representing the transmutations of thought, the interplay of perception and reflection."[1] I. A. Richards felt that "it probably comes nearer to the original Mystery which it perpetuates than transcendentalism does,"[2] and F. R. Leavis asserted that it was "a new start for English poetry."[3] To some extent, all these observations have been shown correct, but it is now much clearer that in technique and method it is a poem much closer to Eliot's early work than to that which followed.

In "Prufrock," as well as in the "Preludes," the images are all contained within the mind of the speaker. Indeed, they come to be extensions of that mind, as in the second of the "Preludes" where

1. *Axel's Castle* (New York, 1931), pp. 107–8.
2. *Principles of Literary Criticism* (New York, 1936), p. 291.
3. *New Bearings in English Poetry* (London, 1932), p. 75.

the speaker's cognition incorporates "all the hands / That are raising dingy shades / In a thousand furnished rooms." There, too, the speaker's soul is entangled with the universe, inseparable from it, "stretched tight across the skies / That fade behind a city block, / Or trampled by insistent feet / At four and five and six o'clock." Consciousness, transposed from image to image, is just as readily given to something inanimate ("a blackened street / Impatient to assume the world") as to sensate creatures. Similarly, in "Rhapsody on a Windy Night," the mind of the speaker shows its ubiquitousness, its ability to assimilate everything unto itself: "Every street lamp that I pass / Beats like a fatalistic drum, / And through the spaces of the dark / Midnight shakes the memory / As a madman shakes a dead geranium." But here the ego, so utterly isolated in Prufrock's case, has undergone a slight expansion. It incorporates at least the mind of the city, with all its sights, sounds, smells. Time, too, has become more fluid and these poems move easily back and forth from present to past to future and back again. As Miller says, "The systematic confusion of times and pronouns confirms the fact that the mind of the protagonist is a collective personality containing all times and persons at once."[4]

This gradual expanding of the ego, incorporating larger and still larger entities, comes to a climax in "Gerontion" and *The Waste Land*. Gerontion is an old man, but his perspective has some limits. His age does not go back to the more remote eras of Western civilization ("I was neither at the hot gates / Nor fought in the warm rain . . ."), but is rather laterally diffused. In his own lifetime he has experienced a sweep of geography, reaching across much of Europe: "My house is a decayed house, / And the jew squats on the window sill, the owner, / Spawned in some estaminet of Antwerp, / Blistered in Brussels, patched and peeled in London" (*CP*, 21). His world is modern Europe, and within that framework he has experienced the decay of his time. His mind encompasses the strangeness of a mixed and fluid world, peopled by the likes of Mr. Silvero, Hakagawa, and Madame de Tornquist. History also has been his lot, but his knowledge of Thermopylae is not first-hand. But in *The Waste Land*, the Gerontion figure is further expanded; Tiresias has been everywhere, seen all, and even views the world from the point of view of both sexes. As an image of the collective mind, Tiresias is the most fully developed figure in Eliot,

4. *Poets*, p. 173.

and since what he "*sees*, in fact, is the substance of the poem" (*CP*, 52), all the allusions and references of *The Waste Land* collect and reverberate within his consciousness.

From the small room of Prufrock's mind, to the city of London in the "Preludes" and "Rhapsody," to the whole of modern Europe in "Gerontion," to, finally, the whole of the experience of Western man, past and present, the subjective ego has moved outward to bring within its reach all of Europe in all times. But the sense of being trapped within narrow limits is still present, and we discover Prufrock abiding in *The Waste Land*:

> I have heard the key
> Turn in the door once and turn once only
> We think of the key, each in his prison
> Thinking of the key, each confirms a prison
> Only at nightfall, aethereal rumours
> Revive for a moment a broken Coriolanus.
>
> (*CP*, 49)

Nor does the ironic view of the early poems disappear in *The Waste Land*. To be sure, the sharply turned, domestic ironies, learned from Laforgue, have given way to larger ones, but from section to section of the poem, event is placed against event, character against character, in such a way as to produce a cumulative effect of overwhelming irony. Even the poem's setting, the city of London (especially the City, the financial district), is exploited for ironic juxtaposition. Some of the ironic allusions, in this regard, are overt, like the reference to Marvell in "at my back from time to time I hear / The sound of horns and motors, which shall bring / Sweeney to Mrs. Porter in the spring" (*CP*, 43). But there are others, more subtle, such as the insensitivity of the bankers moving to work ("And each man fixed his eyes before his feet. / Flowed up the hill and down King William Street . . .") who fail to realize that the bell in Saint Mary Woolnoth sounds the "stroke of nine" not to hasten them into their offices on time, but because the ninth ringing of the bell marks the moment of the elevation of the host in the Eucharist.

Ironic, too, is the use to which the majestic Thames has been put in modern times. Once a place where Elizabeth, in her splendor, could send her barge for Leicester, it is now the scene of a pitiful seduction ("By Richmond I raised my knees / Supine on the floor of a narrow canoe"). And after the event, "He wept. He promised a 'new start' " (*CP*, 46). In the world of the poem, the context for irony is clearly much greater than in any of the earlier works. Past and present are here ironically juxtaposed, and the one such explicit comparison in "Prufrock" (between Prufrock himself and Hamlet) is multiplied and extended.

It is the use of myth, in both "Gerontion" and *The Waste Land*, which points forward to what will be, in "Ash-Wednesday" and *Murder in the Cathedral*, an implementation of ritual materials not only in setting and action, but in the very language as well. In *The Waste Land*, all of history is gathered together and structured in terms of the myth of the Grail quest. Individual events, voices, remain disparate, fragmentary ("These fragments I have shored against my ruins"), but the pieces are all encompassed by the force of the mythic journey of the questing figure seeking purification and release. The quest is itself neither private nor public but both, for as the land is waste because of a falling away from belief, it is redeemable by the representative suffering of the questing figure. Thus the central characters in the poem interfuse with one another, the quest spans time and place, and the identity of the seeker is a collective consciousness in its own right: "Just as the one-eyed merchant . . . melts into the Phoenician Sailor, and the latter is not wholly distinct from Ferdinand Prince of Naples, so all the women are one woman, and the two sexes meet in Tiresias" (*CP*, 52). Since the poet is "*older* than other human beings" (*UPC*, 155), he is able to reach beneath history itself and bring up the fragments which man uses to record history and see them being grouped together into new patterns, new designs. As Miller says, " 'The Waste Land' takes elements from the most diverse times and places . . . and reveals their secret conformity to the universal story . . . found in *From Ritual to Romance*."[5]

At first glance, this use of myth to provide the order for the materials preserved within the collective mind would appear to have solved Eliot's problem of how to get outside the limitation of the self-enclosed ego. By using allusion and myth, Eliot has in *The Waste Land* seemingly discovered a means of compressing all of past time into the short compass of one poem. But, as Miller observes, this "triumph is really defeat," for the quality of the life of the mind of Europe is exactly the same as the experience of the

5. Ibid., p. 177.

solitary ego."[6] And it follows from this that the quest in *The Waste Land* is not completed and fails in the end. The best the poet can do is shore up "fragments . . . against [his] ruins" (*CP*, 50). Rain does not fall, "Hieronymo's mad againe," and the benediction which closes the poem is in a strange, remote, and (to Western minds) unintelligible tongue.

Still, the experiment of *The Waste Land*, with its use of myth and allusion, has been fruitful. If human experience can be patterned by man's mystic projections, then it is equally possible that language itself can, by being ordered into certain patterns, be made to reach out beyond the struggling consciousness; the desire for the wrong thing, which continues to come between man's cognition and the potential "other" which, if it could be reached, might provide restoration. The broken, fragmentary images of *The Waste Land* are signs of language in the throes of a struggle; should that struggle be ended and language made to work less denotatively, by suggestion and even by incantation (as in its liturgical use), then its fragmentary nature might be overcome, and the patterns it describes be a mirror of the larger design which does not depend upon man's individual perception.

It is at this point, between *The Waste Land* and "Ash-Wednesday," that Eliot becomes an avowed Christian. And to be Christian is to deny epistemological idealisms of any sort. The essence of Christian history is rooted in a belief in the *actuality* of the world. The Fall cannot be conceived as something which takes place because of man's perception; it is a result of judgment from without, a placing of an interdiction upon man from beyond his cognition, and it renders him an object, depending upon God's grace for his existence and sustenance. History is real and can be *known* to the Christian view, for only in history as actual event can the relationship between God and man be given any extrinsic meaning. Images of God are not, therefore, mere creations of man's own image-making propensity, but are at worst faint copies of what God introduces into the stream of time and space, at best fair copies of the image of God Himself, as revealed in both the revelation of the Word and the more general, immediate revelation of His created world.

So long as Eliot operates from the point of view of idealist assumptions, God cannot be known except as a projection of man's

6. Ibid., p. 178.

own cognition. With that, history itself must remain, as it does in "Gerontion," something which "issues, deceives with whispering ambitions, / Guides us by vanities." Language, also, for all that lessons from myth and ritual may suggest to the contrary, must remain a matter of self-projection. So long as that is the case, there is no chance that either Prufrock or Gerontion, or even Tiresias, can say anything without the risk of being misunderstood. Words remain frozen within the subjective ego.

But Eliot's conversion to Christianity alters the work which follows. And the difference is not just one of technique, but rather a total difference affecting both style and content. And yet that difference cannot be marked by any radical repudiation of what has preceded it and made the change necessary. There should be no question of Eliot's beginning again, or becoming a totally new poet, unrecognizable in the sound of the earlier voice of "Prufrock" or *The Waste Land*, for to appropriate the theological analogy proper here, to take on a New Nature is not to deny the Old, but rather to see it transformed, redeemed. We should not, therefore, discover in Eliot the kind of change we see in Yeats, where to "descend into the rag and bone-shop of [the] heart"[7] is to seek out a new idiom and thereby to repudiate the old. Rather, we can expect a continual use of already formed materials, only transformed by "a new and shocking / Valuation of all we have been" ("East Coker," *CP*, 125). Carrying the analogy further, we may expect the course of Eliot's poetry, after his conversion, to reflect the larger signification of Christian history with its insistence on the acceptance of the past as something redeemed in every present moment, yet ever pointing to that end which is in fact its beginning. And only in one sense is this a metaphor; at its deepest level it is the actual experience of every Christian life as well as the larger experience of the Christian community as it moves through its ordained history.

Language, too, and Eliot's attitude toward it should reflect this transformation. I have already suggested some of the general ways in which this change is reflected in the criticism of the thirties and early forties. Eliot's increasing interest in the effects of patterns in language, his growing awareness that poetry is made up of words, not only of ideas, emotions, feelings, and his attendant recognition that language may inherently possess structures which in their rhythm and music bear correspondence to the ground of human

7. W. B. Yeats, *Collected Poems* (New York, 1956), p. 335.

emotion, all bear out the fact that the thirties do indeed mark a period of transformation and change in his work. Miller would see the "reversal which makes him a Christian" taking place in his poetry "in the transition from 'The Waste Land' to 'Ash-Wednesday,'" and in that he is correct.[8] But it is first in "Ash-Wednesday" and then in *The Rock* and *Murder in the Cathedral* that the full effect of the change reveals itself.

"Ash-Wednesday" is essentially a poem about humility, the sort of humility which is coincident with a realization that those images which suggest something outside the self are more than mere constructs of the mind. Irony is bred in an atmosphere which God has fled, or from which God has been expelled by man's own enormous capacity to construe everything in terms of himself. There is little or no Christian humility in the small space of Prufrock's world, for there nothing exists but reminders that there is nothing but himself. Understanding must be separated from existence before humility can be expressed, for unless there is something other than man's understanding, there is nothing for him to be humble before.

The humility which is the subject of "Ash-Wednesday" is also evident in the tone of the poem, in its use of language, and in what we might call a new respect for the potentiality of words. The speaker of the poem, the speaker making the resignations, is an emphatic "I," the first such emphatic use of the first person pronoun to appear in any of Eliot's major poems. In this alone much is implied for a new understanding of the role and function of language, for the ability to assert the "I" is at least indicative that the poet no longer feels that personality is merely a matter of point of view. In "Prufrock," as already mentioned, the pronominal world is constantly shifting and there is no clear way to distinguish between the "you" and the "I" of the first line. They could stand for the two aspects of Prufrock's mind or for the speaker (Prufrock?) and his auditor or even for the persona and the poet. They in fact stand for all of these. In that world of subjectivity, names and those terms which take their places are interchangeable. But the "I" of "Ash-Wednesday" is personal, direct, and consistent throughout the poem. Moreover, it is the focus against which other figures take shape. It is the "I" of the poem who speaks to the Lady, who offers the prayers, and who, finally, turns his view to include a larger community, the "us" of the last stanza.

8. *Poets*, p. 179. See also Smidt, *Poetry and Belief*, pp. 191–99.

In one sense, it is a poem which rejects language, for language may, counter to the penitential spirit, be only the assertion of desire. But, of course, no poem can dispense with words, so it is better to say that "Ash-Wednesday" employs language which at points passes into the anonymous language of the Church; it approaches liturgy, and for that reason is very difficult to describe discursively. The extended use of repetitive, incantatory language also renders the poem lyrical, in ways which certainly *The Waste Land* is not. The hardness, the sharpness, and even much of the verbal precision of the former poetry is absent and in its place we find a language almost prosaic at times, frequently abstract, and depending greatly upon simple repetition of phrase and line (the phrase "because I do not hope" or a slight variation of it occurs eleven times in the first thirty-four lines and always at the beginning of the line).

The lines which issue out of the halting beginnings of the first three stanzas ("Because I do not hope to turn again / Because I do not hope / Because I do not hope to turn") become increasingly more complete, and as the poem proceeds, more and more self-contained statements are made. Only the lineation of the first part of section II marks the passage as verse; the sentences follow one another in sequences which are essentially those of rhythmical prose. From out of that ordered syntax, in turn, issues the lyric sung by the bones in the desert (not the "alley" of *The Waste Land* where the "dead men lost their bones"). The lyric itself, part prayer, part liturgical recital, is characterized by paradox, which begins now to take the place of irony:

> End of the endless
> Journey to no end
> Conclusion of all that
> Is inconclusible
> Speech without word and
> Word of no speech
> Grace to the Mother
> For the Garden
> Where all love ends.   (*CP*, 62)

Here, in this one lyric, are gathered a number of Eliot's concerns which will occupy him in the poetry and drama to follow "Ash-Wednesday." Love is here conceived as "itself unmoving / Only the cause and end of movement" ("Burnt Norton," *CP*, 122), and the "hyacinth garden" of unfulfilled human love from *The Waste Land* has become the Garden of Eden and also the garden of the cloister wherein the Virgin invariably finds herself depicted in medieval painting. But the transformation is complex and cannot be spoken of directly. Only paradox can reach, or attempt to reach, that which is already suspected as being beyond the limits of customary language.

Much of the imagery of "Ash-Wednesday" has appeared before in Eliot's poetry, for both *The Waste Land* and "Gerontion" are filled with explicit Christian reference. But in those poems the Christian symbols are either frustrated, or misunderstood by the speaker of the poem. The church of Saint Mary Woolnoth stands like a lonely reminder in the bleak city atmosphere of London, not attended by the hurrying bankers, and beckoning to a people who can no longer read its emblems. Christ "devours" us in "Gerontion" and elsewhere "Signs are taken for wonders." "The word within a word" is "unable to speak a word, / Swaddled with darkness" and the people of the waste land look to arcane and esoteric sources for their understanding. "Madame Sosostris, famous clairvoyante," is "known to be the wisest woman in Europe, / With a wicked pack of cards" even though she "Had a bad cold" (*CP*, 38). The "chapel" is empty, "only the wind's home. / It has no windows, and the door swings," for "Dry bones can harm no one" (*CP*, 49). In these poems the religious symbols, particularly the Christian, stand out sharply against a background of darkness, waste, and isolation. They are at best only remotely fused with the secular images which surround them and, ultimately, no one in the context of those poems understands their relevance.

But in "Ash-Wednesday" this symbolic material, already discovered amidst the desolation of the empty waste land of the earlier poetry, is given a new role and is made to form an inextricable part of the entire context of the poem. The effect is startling, for rather than the religious images standing out from their surroundings, the secular images are made to take on a religious sense. To Allen Tate, it is "evident that Eliot has hit upon the only method now available of using the conventional religious image in poetry" by reducing it from symbol to image, "from abstraction to the plane of sensation."[9] What actually Eliot has hit upon is the fact of Incarnation, and it is

9. "On *Ash-Wednesday*," in *T. S. Eliot: The Man and His Work*, p. 135.

that which makes it possible for him to deal in seemingly abstract terms and produce the effect of rendering sensation. It is the Incarnation which makes possible the "new years" which restore "With a new verse the ancient rhyme" (CP, 64). No longer is the collective mind, the mind of Europe, a projection of the self, but the self has become an instrument of the collective mind. By listening, rather than by asserting, the poet can perhaps "Redeem / The unread vision in the higher dream / While jewelled unicorns draw by the gilded hearse" (CP, 64). Nor does "redeem" here mean to gain back lost time or to recapture the past. Its sense is the same as when Prince Hal speaks of redeeming the time in I Henry IV; it means making the most of every moment, both by action and by waiting without anxiety, as the moment might require. It requires that one recognize a pattern not of his own construction and have the will to place himself within that pattern, even though its shape not be clearly discernible.

Redemption of time is also a redemption of language. No longer conceived as the arbitrary marker of human cognition but as an instrument of revelation, springing from without the limitations of the self, language can be freed from its bondage to the subjective mind and can explore new paths. Poetry can be written in new ways because all ways are already determined in the structure of the language itself; it is therefore the poet's task to fit himself into the patterns of his language and bring to light those designs which are potentially there, contained in the mind of God. Poetry is what *realizes* the shape of human experience, gives it order and meaning, not something which makes experience or creates a world apart from the already existing one. It may even be capable of recapturing the lost word which is the revelation of God in history, that is to say, the revelation of Incarnation:

> If the lost word is lost, if the spent word is spent
> If the unheard, unspoken
> Word is unspoken, unheard;
> Still is the unspoken word, the Word unheard,
> The Word without a word, the Word within
> The world and for the world;
> And the light shone in darkness and
> Against the Word the unstilled world still whirled
> About the centre of the silent Word.   (CP, 65)

The effect of the word "still" at the beginning of the fourth line is striking and suggests much of what the entire passage is about, namely, the stillness within which one must wait for the sound of the word which is spoken from without. In order to hear the "Word without a word" all other words have to be silenced. But the "still" has also the other meaning of "yet," of something which continues in spite of the inattention of the world. The double meaning of the word, its crucial placement in the passage, and its referring both to what precedes and what follows it can be seen as a paradigm of at least one of the ways in which Eliot was coming to learn to use language to utter the unutterable. It gains meaning also from its being repeated, in slightly different context, in the "unstilled" and "still whirled" of the next to the last line in the stanza. It points forward to that major image of stasis-in-motion which plays a vital part in the meaning of both *Murder in the Cathedral* and *Four Quartets*—the still point of the ever turning cosmos, or the center of the turning wheel.

The world of subjectivity is not altogether absent from "Ash-Wednesday," as the ironic first stanza indicates. But it is nonetheless in the process of being denied, and the course of the poem is the working out of that process. While the self is still self-centered in the first stanza, the last section of the poem provides a vision of the world without, that world of phenomenal reality which is almost always subjectivized in the earlier poetry. The speaker sees, from the "wide window" of the staircase he has been climbing, a view of the "the hawthorn blossom and a pasture scene," "the granite shore / The white sails . . . seaward, seaward flying / Unbroken wings" (*CP*, 63, 66). The "lost heart" (like the "vanished power of the usual reign")

> rejoices
> In the lost lilac and the lost sea voices
> And the weak spirit quickens to rebel
> For the bent golden-rod and the lost sea smell
> Quickens to recover
> The cry of quail and the whirling plover
> And the blind eye creates
> The empty forms between the ivory gates
> And smell renews the salt savour of the sandy earth.
>
> (*CP*, 66)

This is very close to the concreteness of William Carlos Williams and strikes a new note in Eliot's poetry. The world outside is here affirmed, accepted as being just that—outside the limits of human subjectivizing. The spirit can "quicken" with this realization, it can take on new life and even rejoice that the lilac of nostalgia and memory have been lost. The images in this passage are ones which immediately appeal to the senses, yet their context has already given them a religious connotation. Incarnation is revealed not only in the accepted signs of the faith, but in the natural world and all its aspects as well.

Other poems of the period repeat this note of rejoicing in having discovered the "other" against which man may judge his existence. The "scent of pine and the woodthrush singing through the fog" in "Marina" and the "running stream and a water-mill beating the darkness" of "Journey of the Magi" all testify to this new awareness that there is a world of actuality which lies beyond the power of man's image-making grasp. Personally, privately at least, the poet has come into a new possession and the way is open out of the "Streets that follow like a tedious argument / Of insidious intent." Through humility, and by denying the very things which language generally strives to assert, namely human will and desire, Eliot has come to a new perspective from which it will naturally follow that he will work to render his personal vision of reality a public one, which can be shared by the community.

The first stage in this expansion takes place in *The Rock*, the pageant-play Eliot wrote on commission for the Forty-Five Churches Fund of the Diocese of London in 1934.[10] As drama, it leaves much to be desired, but then it was not designed exclusively as a dramatic entertainment, but rather as a series of scenes which unfold the struggle of a community to find within itself the means and the motivation to erect a cathedral. But though the whole of the pageant is certainly unsatisfying, the choruses frequently rise above the topical level of the rest of the scenario, and it is in the choruses that he displays most clearly some as yet experimental techniques.

In places, the chorus of workmen chants verses which recall the lyric contained in "Ash-Wednesday":

10. Not all of the project was Eliot's design. The scenario was written by E. Martin Browne, and it is likely that some of the speeches were the result of hands other than Eliot's. See D. E. Jones, *The Plays of T. S. Eliot* (London, 1960), pp. 38–40.

> *The river flows, the seasons turn,*
> *The sparrow and starling have no time to waste.*
> *If men do not build*
> *How shall they live?*
> *When the field is tilled*
> *And the wheat is bread*
> *They shall not die in a shortened bed*
> *And a narrow sheet.* (CP, 99)

What men do is here a mirror of what the creatures of the wood do, and man's time for building is measured by the change of seasons and the example of the field. No longer is the whole world an extension of man's thinking, but man is conceived as the major entity among a world of separate yet correspondent entities. The meaning of life can be structured into it by recognizing that what the natural order does in its way, man can emulate in his. In such a fashion as this were generations of the past granted continuity, and the effort of common man understood to be an image of the labor of the saints of God, and His acts of building:

> Thus your fathers were made
> Fellow citizens of the saints, of the household of GOD, being
>   built upon the foundation
> Of apostles and prophets, Christ Jesus Himself the chief
>   cornerstone. (CP, 100)

It was only after man had convinced himself that the architecture of the world was really of his own design that the building, with its intricate and mutually supporting girders, began to come apart. Man erred most in presuming to define God. The long process which issued from man's first desire to fix "the place of GOD, / And [settle] all the inconvenient saints" finds its culmination in the condition which Prufrock inherits: a world where God is dead and nothing exists on the limitless horizon but the projections of man's own thinking. Something of material gain and perhaps even something of an intellectual advancement has marked the process, but the final result sees much "left at home unsure" since home in such a boundless world is itself hard to locate.

One of the chief values of Eliot's experiment in *The Rock* was to explore the possibilities of a new verse form for dramatic purposes. The language of the choruses is close to that of everyday speech in its diction, but remote from it in its use of repetition and iteration. What gives many of the choruses the quality of speech is the use of stress rather than syllabic count to determine the length of each line. Line length approaches that of contemporary prose, while the adherence to a pattern of stress retains the sense of regularity and rhythm required to make the whole verse, and differentiate it from prose. But, as D. E. Jones points out, the full effect of this experiment is not entirely realized in *The Rock*, largely because that work lacks a unifying dramatic conception.[11] It will show itself to best effect in the major work which was to follow, *Murder in the Cathedral*. There, the uniting of a cohesive dramatic structure, a verse form approximating the natural rhythms of common speech, and, most importantly, a conviction that language can be made to serve communicative ends forms what is perhaps the most successful of Eliot's ventures into drama. Having found a language useful for public presentation, Eliot is able to fashion a plan which is emphatically about the concerns of his own time transmitted in verbal terms which render its assertions universal.

Miller writes, "The human body and the world's body—these are two forms of incarnation. Another is that social form of embodiment which is a man's acceptance of a limited role in his community. This theme is central in Eliot's plays. *Murder in the Cathedral* associates it explicitly with the Incarnation."[12] What ultimately tempts Becket is the very thing which had so constricted the early Eliot and which is a constant lure of Christianity, namely, a hope that one can attain a spiritual state purely, without being dirtied by the world's goods. It is analogous to the last and great temptation proffered Christ by the Devil in the desert—the promise of being the object of all adulation rather than serving as a mere subject of God's. The promise offered by the Fourth Tempter moves on two levels, the secular and the spiritual. In the secular realm, Thomas is told he already holds the balance of power, would he but exercise it; yet the crowning temptation is not temporal:

> But think, Thomas, think of glory after death.
> When king is dead, there's another king,
> And one more king is another reign. (*CP*, 191)

11. Ibid., pp. 48–49.
12. *Poets*, p. 185. By "acceptance of a limited role in . . . community" is not meant, here, a small as opposed to a large role, but rather a role of any sort as opposed to none.

The world as seen by the Fourth Tempter is all illusion, and within his understanding, he describes it with telling accuracy. It is a world where nothing holds, and where all is fiction generated by man's cognition. Since that is so, his offer is sincere by his lights, for Thomas would be denying nothing but the shape of his own dreams to forego the world and seek spiritual perfection in martyrdom.

The Tempter tells Thomas:

> You have also thought, sometimes at your prayers,
> Sometimes hesitating at the angles of stairs,
> And between sleep and waking . . .
> That nothing lasts, but the wheel turns,
> The nest is rifled, and the bird mourns.
>
> (CP, 192)

Since all this world is subjectivity, nothing in it can be of any permanent value and the way history will recall the martyr will be only a function of its own needs for self-justification:

> And later is worse, when men will not hate you
> Enough to defame or to execrate you,
> But pondering the qualities that you lacked
> Will only try to find the historical fact.
> When men shall declare that there was no mystery
> About this man who played a certain part in history.
>
> (CP, 192)

And Thomas' question to this, asking whether "there [is] no enduring crown to be won," sets up the central concern of the play. Should the Fourth Tempter prove right, and the world reveal itself as illusion and subjective projection, then to accept his offer would gain only the extension of that illusion into a higher realm. But, on the other hand, should the Tempter prove wrong, and the world show itself as a place of actuality where action implies responsibility to others, how can one differentiate between what his own, self-enclosed will desires and what some larger, external Power might wish? Is it not, after all, a matter of words? Perhaps how one puts the question is what determines the shape of the answer, and is it possible to know that anything exists other than what one thinks? It is the tempter himself who says "I am only here, Thomas, to tell you what you know" (CP, 191).

But the Fourth Tempter condescends, and considers the creatures of the world as dust, not worth Thomas' anguish. His appeal is direct:

> Seek the way of martyrdom, make yourself the lowest
> On earth, to be high in heaven.
> And see far off below you, where the gulf is fixed,
> Your persecutors, in timeless torment,
> Parched passion, beyond expiation.
> (CP, 192–93)

To accept this sort of temptation would be to accept the very kind of world which Eliot himself has been at pains to escape. It would be to put Thomas in the Prufrockian situation.

Thomas' rejection of the temptation to accept the world as "a cheat and a disappointment" is the center of the play, and it is expressed most completely in the sermon he delivers on Christmas morning. He tells his community that a martyrdom "is always . . . the design of God, for His love of men, to warn them and to lead them, to bring them back to His ways. . . . the true martyr is he who has become the instrument of God, who has lost his will in the will of God . . . [and who] no longer desires anything for himself, not even the glory of martyrdom" (CP, 199–200). It is in a prose both measured and simple, making use of contemporary idiom to render concrete some ideas which are difficult to grasp because they are essentially abstract. The language of this sermon owes something to the practice of Bishop Andrewes, whom Eliot had discussed in a 1926 essay. Andrewes' habit was to explore the meanings of a single word, working it through a number of contexts until it could be revealed in "lucid profundity." And to the reader willing to follow the turns of the Bishop's thought, the result will be clarity and a new understanding, for "Andrewes takes a word and derives the world from it; squeezing the word until it yields a full juice of meaning which we should never have supposed any word to possess" (SE, 347–48). It is just this process of "squeezing the word" which Eliot presents us with in Thomas' sermon, for the word *martyrdom* is there considered in a variety of contexts and is made to yield meanings which go beyond those affixed to it by either the people of Canterbury or the knights who come to kill the Archbishop. The process of the prose is marked by what Eliot calls, elsewhere, "ordonance and precision," and it is just those qualities which the justifying speeches of the knights, near the close of the play, lack.

The play gives us, then, examples of both the new sort of dramatic verse Eliot had experimented with in *The Rock* and the kind of prose which forces meaning out of particular terms, even the specialized vernaculars of modern society. Of the latter, the play also presents examples, and the speeches of the knights as they plead their case are brilliant instances of contemporary prose caught in the mesh of legal jargon. In the language of the chorus Eliot has discovered a way of treating dogma in the context of actual lives, so that the effect of what the women of Canterbury say is to make the audience accept them as believable people, even though they are testifying to a Christian interpretation of the nature of history. To take just one example, in the litany sung at the close of the play, the blending of the commonplace with the exalted, the daily idiom with the liturgical rhythm, achieves, as Eliot nowhere before had achieved, the mixture of common speech which articulates experience with speech which enacts a ritual pattern. It is the pattern as much as the parts that constitute it that enforces the meaning; the language of tradition serves the idiom of the present. Word and deed, for the people of Canterbury as for the Archbishop himself, have been brought very close to one another.

Here, in *Murder in the Cathedral,* Incarnation has been centered upon a historical event and been contained within a dramatic framework. Action imitating action gives a credibility even to those things which are in fact mysterious, for the stage is first of all a place where we *see* something. Having found a language to treat the mysterious in dramatic terms, the question remains whether Eliot can use the same language to effect similar ends in the non-dramatic shape of his poetry.

4

The Romantic Inheritance Overcome

the communication
Of the dead is tongued with fire
beyond the language of the
living

AFTER 1935, Eliot's poetry and drama are everywhere filled with the realizations of an external reality, but the cost of the struggle to achieve that realization in poetry is still very much a burden to Eliot. Somehow, somewhere, something had gone wrong with the course of European and English sensibility and the result had been, in Eliot's view, both a mistaken understanding of the world and an attendant deterioration in language. He had first described the problem at the same time as he was setting forth his program for poetry, itself based on the assumption of a continuity in tradition and literary usage. In the famous essay of 1921 on the metaphysical poets, Eliot had explained how the "poets of the seventeenth century, the successors of the dramatists of the sixteenth, possessed a mechanism of sensibility which could devour any kind of experience" (*SE*, 287). These poets were "simple, artificial, difficult, or fantastic, as their predecessors were; no less nor more than Dante, Guido Cavalcanti, Guinicelli, or Cino" (*SE*, 287–88). But, alas, something has gone wrong and sometime in the "seventeenth century a dissociation of sensibility set in, from which we have never recovered" (*SE*, 288). Needless to say, the concept logically conflicts with his idea of an unbroken tradition as he explains it in "Tradition and the Individual Talent." But it seems to have had the more lasting appeal, for in 1936 we find him extending his 1921 castigation of Milton and virtually laying the blame for the "dissociation of sensibility" at his feet. The influence of Milton on succeeding generations of poets was all the greater because Milton was a great poet, and therefore the particular deterioration to which he subjected the language all the more difficult to overcome: "Many people will agree that a man may be a great artist, and yet have a bad influence. There is more of Milton's influence in the badness of the bad verse of the eighteenth century than of anybody's else: he certainly did more harm than Dryden and Pope, and perhaps a good deal of the obloquy which has fallen on these two poets . . . ought to be transferred to Milton" (*OP*, 156–57). Most of the rest of the essay is unfortunate, as Eliot himself came to realize later. But though we can deplore the tone of his remarks, particularly those regarding Milton's blindness ("The most important fact about Milton, for my purpose, is his blindness"), taken together they remind us of how important Eliot deemed it to find some cause for that "dissociation of sensibility" he discovered setting in sometime in the seventeenth century.

The essay is important also because it reveals another tension in Eliot's definition of poetry. In the 1933 lecture on Arnold, as we have seen, Eliot decried that poet's lack of what he called the "auditory imagination." Now, in 1936, Milton is faulted because he lacked "visual imagination." In Milton's verse the "syntax is deter-mined by the musical significance, by the auditory imagination, rather than by the attempt to follow actual speech or thought. . . . The result with Milton is, in one sense of the word, *rhetoric.* . . . This kind of 'rhetoric' is not necessarily bad in its influence; but it may be considered bad in relation to the historical life of a language as a whole." The real trouble with Milton, in this regard, is that he did not help in preserving "the tradition of conversational language in poetry" (*OP*, 161). On the one hand, Eliot would see language as part of the collective mind of tradition, fixed and transmitted intact from generation to generation of poets; on the other, he would view it as something which can share in and reflect a shift in cultural and epistemological orientation and hence as something which can be damaged by wrong handling. The first attitude is prescriptive and is of a piece with Eliot's early enthusiasm for clas-sicist, authoritarian ideas. The second is descriptive and reflects Eliot's gradually emerging sense of social change and cultural decay. Or so it seems on the surface. But the fact is that even the latter view is prescriptive, for to assume that language can deteriorate by misuse is to assume that there is a language in ideal shape against which such deterioration can be measured. Though the two views are, in that sense, close to one another, the fact remains that to Eliot there appeared a difficulty in reconciling them.

I have suggested that the reconciliation is partly achieved through the experimentation in the poetry and drama of the thirties, but the theoretical background for that Eliot had suggested earlier, as early in fact as 1919, in his first essay on *Hamlet*. There, in attempting to discover what was the matter with the play (as he saw it), he declared his now well-known idea of the "objective correlative." For someone caught in the midst of a subjective world, trying to find a means of uniting word and thing, his very choice of terms is significant. For emotion to be adequately expressed in art, he says, one must find an " 'objective correlative'; in other words, a set of objects, a situation, a chain of events which shall be the formula of that *particular* emotion; such that when the external facts, which must terminate in sensory experience, are given, the emotion is immediately evoked" (*SE*, 145). All of these terms—"set of objects, a situation, a chain of events"—are considered as "external facts," and though they are understood to terminate in "sensory experience" they are not the same thing as that experience. And here we have one of the first instances where Eliot makes a move to separate understanding from existence. It will not, however, be until nearly a decade later that a satisfactory correlative will present itself to Eliot, one that by its total view of the world makes and attempts to enforce such a distinction. I am speaking here of Christianity, for it is that which becomes for Eliot the most valuable "objective correlative" and which, assimilated into the poetry, will provide the separation of internal from external so longed for by the early Eliot.

Though he does not again refer to the term "objective correlative" after 1919, except now and again to express surprise at the currency the phrase came to have, his 1930 essay on Baudelaire (which repeats many of the things he had said earlier about the French poet) implies throughout that one of that poet's chief gifts was his having a sense of something external to himself by which to give point and object to his intentions. And Baudelaire is admired also because he was a rebel against the very ideas which Eliot himself had been struggling to overcome. Baudelaire, like Eliot, was "inevitably the offspring of romanticism, and by his nature the first counter-romantic in poetry . . ." (*SE*, 424). He "perceived that what really matters is Sin and Redemption" (*SE*, 427) and that perception made it possible for him to reach out toward "something which cannot be had *in*, but which may be had partly *through*, personal relations" (*SE*, 427–28).[1]

1. Eliot goes on, in the same place, to say, "Indeed, in much romantic poetry the sadness is due to the exploitation of the fact that no human relations are

Baudelaire's understanding that there was something outside himself to which he could relate made it possible for him to be a poet of salvation, a poet Christian in the best sense, whose business is not necessarily to practice Christianity, but "to assert its *necessity*" (*SE*, 422). The effect of this understanding is most markedly shown by what Baudelaire achieved in language. Accepting the fact of Sin was also to accept the fact of commonplace ugliness, of the life of the city with all its squalor, even of the depravity of human existence, and to be able thereby to make a truly contemporary poetry which spoke the idiom of his time and place. By seeing the world as a place of actuality, not as something mentally projected or as merely a state of mind, and by using the materials of that world, Baudelaire was able to speak through the commonplace (the notion of a transparent language) and make it "represent something much more than itself" (*SE*, 426). In short, Baudelaire's poetry reached out for the Absolute by means of a celebration of the present in all its conditions, by means of a celebration of the here and now. This is precisely what Eliot's major work beginning with "Ash-Wednesday" attempts to do.

But we can ask ourselves here about the outcome of Eliot's remarks concerning the auditory and the visual imagination. How do they come to be reconciled? The answer is both simple and complex. Once Christianity becomes the overreaching "objective correlative," the theoretical concerns which occupy much of Eliot's early discussion of the nature of poetry cease to be relevant—as theory. Once an Absolute has been proclaimed, there is no need to ascertain discursively the truth about good or bad poetry, for now one need only assert, or argue by extension. A moral order being discovered external to the self renders criticism a part of that order, and the critical task is no longer merely aesthetic, but also moral. As Vincent Buckley has pointed out, the later criticism of Eliot, "at least" that from 1932, "is less concerned to affirm impersonality than to pass censure on the literary uses of personality. It reveals an open moral concern, even a moralistic one; for Eliot is . . . interested . . . to find some means of protecting the modern sensibility against certain unhealthy factors as they receive a literary form in contemporary novels and poems. . . . His concern is

---

adequate to human desires, but also to the *disbelief in any further object for human desires than that which, being human, fails to satisfy them*" (italics mine).

pastoral."[2] Nowhere is this more forcibly expressed than in the 1935 essay "Religion and Literature." Since "the whole of modern literature is corrupted by what I call Secularism, that it is simply unaware of, simply cannot understand the meaning of, the primacy of the supernatural over the natural life . . . literary criticism should be completed from a definite ethical and theological standpoint" (SE, 398, 388).

That Eliot came to reconcile his variant views regarding meaning and style, or regarding the visual and the auditory imagination, can be seen from a series of remarks which appear in the criticism from 1933 through 1946. In 1933, he was still in places disparaging meaning as the most relevant aspect of poetry.[3] But in "The Music of Poetry" he brings the two, sound (or music) and meaning, together and recognizes them as a unity: "But I would remind you, first, that the music of poetry is not something which exists apart from the meaning" (OP, 21). And shortly after this comes a passage which is remarkable for the number of ways it indicates Eliot's transformed understanding of language, and particularly the peculiar language of poetry—a transformation which had been in process throughout the better part of a decade. Since it has much bearing on the poems which he had just completed (the Quartets) it will bear quoting here in full:

We have still a good way to go in the invention of a verse medium for the theatre, a medium in which we shall be able to hear the speech of contemporary human beings, in which dramatic characters can express the purest poetry without high-falutin and in which they can convey the most commonplace message without absurdity. But when we reach a point at which the poetic idiom can be stabilized, then a period of musical elaboration can follow. I think that a poet may gain much from the study of music . . . the properties in which music concerns the poet most nearly, are the sense of rhythm and the sense of structure. I think that it might be possible for a poet to work too closely to musical analogies . . . but I know that a poem, or a passage of a poem, may tend to realize itself first as a particular rhythm before it reaches expression in words, and that this rhythm may bring to birth the idea and

2. *Poetry and Morality* (London, 1961), p. 129.
3. *UPC*, p. 15.

the image. . . . The use of recurrent themes is as natural to
poetry as to music (*OP*, 32).

Here, discursively, we are given all the major concerns of Eliot's
later poetry: the emphasis on pattern and design, the analogy from
music, the idea that meaning may be achieved through repetition
and recurrence of rhythmic and verbal patterns. But the question
remains, how do these concerns, essentially a transformed view of
language, affect the poetry itself?

The *Quartets* are preoccupied with the Christian doctrine of time
and eternity, and like all Eliot's work beginning with "Ash-
Wednesday," they presuppose the possibility of man's ability to
possess a physical world external to himself and having a life of its
own. Their central theme is, in Miller's terms, the "abnegation of
any humanly imposed pattern in order to recover the divine pattern."[4] To this end, the poet must forego his earlier attempt to unify
disparate elements into a new whole, for the locus of unity has been
shifted; it no longer is seen to rest in man's cognition but rather is
discovered in the external world which is unified through God.
Since the real pattern of history is God's, man's attempt to overcome his own temporal or spatial condition by imposing his own
patterns upon experience can only result in a perversion of the
larger, encompassing design of which he is but a part. The way of
illumination must therefore involve the way of self-negation and
self-denial, for "hope would be hope for the wrong thing" and "love
would be love of the wrong thing" ("East Coker," *CP*, 126). In
order truly to overcome time, one must submit to time, for only in
the patterns of memory can the "moment in the rose-garden, / The
moment in the arbour where the rain beat. / The moment in the
draughty church at smokefall / Be remembered" ("Burnt Norton,"
CP, 119–20). Through submission to memory and the patterns which
can be recalled thereby, a timeless reality can from time to time
be apprehended, felt in time, and remembered in time. Such an
experience can only be explained by theology, for it is the experience upon which religion builds a discipline.

There are two views of time which stand in opposition to that
which the *Quartets* express. One of these, and one which the poems
treat in several places, sees time as an endless process from which
there can be no escape. "Burnt Norton" opens with this concept of
time hypothetically stated:

4. *Poets*, p. 187.

Time present and time past
Are both perhaps present in time future,
And time future contained in time past.
If all time is eternally present
All time is unredeemable. (*CP*, 117)

Since redemption requires that there be possibility of change, no past error can be corrected in a timeless present and "What might have been is an abstraction / Remaining a perpetual possibility / Only in a world of speculation" (*CP*, 117). This is the condition in which Prufrock labors to effect some communication. In his ever present time enclosure, nothing can be said that would matter and no action is possible, for action requires that there be movement and movement presupposes change. Time is real in this view, frighteningly so, for there is nothing but time and only man's capacity for making images of himself can relieve the ennui which results from such an environment. The temptation to do just that had been faced by Eliot much earlier, and even now, in the *Quartets*, the lure of that particular brand of idealism still has its attractions. But the poems move to reject this view.

The other, more subtle concept of time which the *Quartets* treat understands temporality as illusion, and suggests that the way of escaping the illusion is by escaping the world itself, which is the great receptacle of that illusion. This is essentially the understanding of time which marks most Eastern religious thought, and it tempts the speaker in the *Quartets*. But this notion, like the first, is ultimately rejected, and the Christian concept of time as both a matter of the present and a matter of eternity pervades the poems. Since, in a sense, the Christian concept of time incorporates both of the others, it is not because of any mere desire to increase the scope of the poems that Eliot treats all three. Since for Christians history is the place of intersection between time and eternity, the pervading sense of time in the poems is closely connected with historical events.

In the first place, the poems derive from aspects of Eliot's own personal history. Burnt Norton is a country house in Gloucestershire where Eliot had stayed as a visitor in 1934; East Coker is a village in Somersetshire from which the Eliot family emigrated to America; the Dry Salvages are "a small group of rocks, with a beacon, off the N.E. coast of Cape Ann, Massachusetts" (*CP*, 130) which Eliot remembered from summers spent there in his childhood; Little Gidding, in Huntingdonshire, visited by Eliot in 1936, was the location of a religious community established in 1625 by Nicolas Ferrar and later visited three times by King Charles.[5] Not only had Eliot some personal connection with each of these places, that is to say a direct relationship, but three of them relate to him through more than one way. His youth spent in summer months on Cape Ann recalls the context of his immediate family, his mother and father; East Coker recalls the whole of the Eliot family and serves to remind that one of Eliot's English ancestors was Sir Thomas Ellyott; Little Gidding, with its Anglican associations, recalls Eliot's own conversion and the earlier history of his family, some of whom had been among the first members of the Anglican community in England. There can be no such thing as an isolated history; since history is a process and ongoing, one's own life is but a mirror and paradigm of the lives preceding it and from which it issues. Almost immediately, private becomes public and the singular, communal.

The events which constitute history can be known through memory, and none better than those which have played a direct part in shaping one's own personal memory. Whereas Prufrock is a persona from necessity (in the world of utter subjectivity, there can be only personae, no real identities), the speaker of the *Quartets* is "I," the Eliot who is both poet in his time and a man in the process of history. As in "Ash-Wednesday," there is no longer any need for the Tiresias figure, since the poet himself, utilizing his own memory to unlock the collective memory of his history, his race, can serve the same function. Moreover, it is necessary that the "I" be speaker, for the undertaking of these poems is nothing less than a spiritual journey, which, like Dante's, can only be performed by submitting to the suffering required to wrestle words into place—the poet thereby restores to himself a role once traditional in Western poetry, that of pastor and prophet.

To achieve the end of freeing memory from the concerns of the moment, the distractions of the hour, recourse is made to patterns, and the *Quartets* are filled with various patterns. Not only is the idea of pattern itself mentioned frequently, but the whole of the four poems are interrelated in such a way as to provide a rough approximation of the structure of the musical sonata form. But it

5. Grover Smith, T. S. *Eliot's Poetry and Plays* (Chicago, 1960), p. 255.

is in the verse itself that the most conspicuous use of patterning is made, for in these poems Eliot refines his experiments with stress verse to achieve what is probably the nearest thing in contemporary poetry to the alliterative verse of the late Middle Ages. As Helen Gardner has ably demonstrated, Eliot employs three basic stress groupings and uses them as a base for a variety of modulations.[6] Of the three (Gardner distinguishes a four-stress line, a three-stress line, and a six-stress line as the basic patterns), the predominant one throughout the four poems is the four-stress line with which "Burnt Norton" opens. The stress in these lines is accompanied by overt alliteration, yet the amount of variety Eliot achieves in both stress and alliteration makes the result a matter of great subtlety. The frequent monotony of much alliterative verse is thereby overcome and in its place we are given a verse which seems free yet is in fact highly structured and shaped. Within this verse Eliot is at liberty to make use of commonplace speech, sententious diction, colloquial diction, and, in short, the entire gamut of language as it is spoken and written. Gardner has characterized it as "metrical speech" and the phrase is appropriate. She goes on to say that the "supreme merit of his verse, however, is the liberty it has given him to include every variety of diction, and to use the poetic as boldly as the prosaic, without any restraint. It has enabled him also to express his own vision of life in a form in which that vision can be perfectly embodied."[7]

The yearning after the apprehension of the eternal which is so much a part of the *Quartets* demands more than metrical flexibility, however. If words are to be made to reach across the void, to explore the "frontiers of consciousness," then not only must metrical facility be exploited, but also the customary vehicle of poetry, namely, the metaphorical. For however much the poems acknowledge the existence of an actual world existing apart from the perceiving self, that alone is not sufficient to transfix the "still point of the turning world" which is "Neither flesh nor fleshless; / Neither from nor towards" (*CP*, 119). For that task, if indeed it can be accomplished, the metaphorical basis of the poetry must be made to carry a weight not customarily associated with metaphor. For Dante, the difficulty was not so great, for he had an accepted allegorical practice at his disposal (a typical fifteenth-century defi-

6. *The Art of T. S. Eliot,* pp. 25–35.
7. P. 35.

nition of allegory held that it was continued metaphor) which could be immediately understood by his readers. The allegorical framework, coupled with an amazing ability to select the most appropriate imagery, made it possible for Dante to express "experience so remote from ordinary experience" (*SE*, 267) that few poets have even attempted anything similar to his undertaking.

But allegory, at least as Dante employed it, is no longer a usable vehicle for the poet, and so the effect it earlier had can no longer be achieved in that way (the "allegory . . . makes it possible for the reader who is not even a good Italian scholar to enjoy Dante. Speech varies, but our eyes are all the same" [*SE*, 243]). What is required is some manner of giving voice to the experience often called mystical, without having recourse to the subjective devices of, say, Wordsworth. "For most of us, there is only the unattended / Moment, the moment in and out of time, / The distraction fit, lost in a shaft of sunlight" (*CP*, 136), and poetry can reveal such moments. "But to apprehend / The point of intersection of the timeless / With time, is an occupation for the saint— / No occupation either, but something given / And taken, in a lifetime's death in love, / Ardour and selflessness and self-surrender" (*CP*, 136). To achieve that end is to try to make poetry go beyond the realm of poetry, to make language perform the task of rendering mystical insight.

Eliot ranges over a wide area of mystical thought in the *Quartets*, bringing together fragments and allusions from the *Bhagavad-Gita* as well as from Christian mystics such as Dame Juliana of Norwich and St. John of the Cross. Behind much of the mystical material of the poems lie the spirits of Plato, Plotinus, and Heraclitus. Such diversity has been criticized by some as a blemish on what appears to be the predominantly Christian movement throughout these poems. Helen Gardner takes particular issue with the inclusion of references to the *Gita* in "The Dry Salvages."[8] But such a criticism misses the point, for it fails to recognize the common ground behind the mystical thought of all religions, and perhaps of primitive myth as well. There is a point on the ladder of mystical illumination shared by all mystical experience, regardless of whether it be had by a Christian, a Hindu, or a Buddhist. Evelyn Underhill states this commonality of mysticism in these terms: "It denies that possible knowledge is to be limited (a) to sense impressions, (b) to any

8. P. 173*n*.

process of intellection, (c) to the unfolding of the content of normal consciousness. . . . The mystics find the basis of their method not in logic but in life; in the existence of a discoverable 'real,' a spark of true being, within the seeking subject, which can, in the ineffable experience which they call the 'act of union,' fuse itself with and thus apprehend the reality of the sought object."[9] The "occupation for the saint" is equatable with the mystic's communion with the "sought object" and the many allusions throughout the *Quartets* establish an extended pattern of references to other times and places where to some such a communion has come. Though the personal tone is present throughout much of the *Quartets*, we need not make Eliot any sort of mystical seer; the experience which comes to the mystic is simply the most intense Eliot could employ for his own attempt to reach beyond the limits of sequential language. The awareness of the personal dimension serves, however, to increase this intensity. We are aware that Little Gidding was a place of spiritual communion in the sixteenth century, but that realization is made more poignant with the knowledge that Eliot himself visited (and perhaps worshipped) there. Prayer, also, is a personal matter, and each of the four poems contains a prayer.

But it is largely on the metaphorical level that the *Quartets* aim "beyond language." Utilizing complex juxtapositions and extended comparisons, many metaphors in these poems attempt to subsume various feelings and experiences into a new unity, while maintaining the integrity of the parts; Eliot has enlarged and extended the metaphysical "conceit."[10]

The rose-garden of "Burnt Norton" is an example. On one level, it is merely a place recalled as a spot one had visited. There is some suggestion that the place was associated with a significant experience, now all but forgotten in the dimness of the past. Yet the speaker was warned away, for it was a place of too much reality

9. *Mysticism* (New York, 1956), p. 24.

10. Perhaps it is instructive to note, in this regard, that much of the work of a significant number of postwar British poets, particularly those associated with the Movement, is characterized by a studious avoidance of metaphor. For most of them, concerned as they are with recording the mundane and commonplace in human experience, metaphor implies both an unwanted debt to such poets as Eliot and an unwise attempt to transcend their (as they see it) limited condition. Robert Conquest, introducing his anthology of 1956, comments on the "wide acceptance" gained during the thirties and forties of the "debilitating theory that poetry *must* be metaphorical." See *New Lines*, ed. Robert Conquest (London, 1956), p. xii.

and "human kind / Cannot bear very much reality" (*CP*, 118). It was also a paradoxical location where there was "unheard music hidden in the shrubbery, / And the unseen eyebeam crossed" and it had been reached by "the passage which we did not take" (*CP*, 118, 117). What sort of metaphorical significance can this place have, introduced as it is by paradox and left with a suggestion that it embodied some revelation more real than human kind can bear? There is certainly some association of the image with a place of sensual love, and the rose is also a traditional Christian symbol for the Virgin. Moreover, throughout the Middle Ages, the customary representation of the Virgin Annunciate placed her in an enclosed garden. In addition, the "lotus" of the episode carries with it certain quasi-mystical Hindu associations and, in the *Odyssey*, is related to the realm of dreams.[11] The suggestion of a dream sequence is heightened by the uncertain identity of the children and their relationship to the garden. The entire passage draws together a variety of allusions and connotations, yet never completely subsumes them into a new and homogeneous whole. The various elements of the garden metaphor exist independently in the whole, informing it and adding to its meaning, but never becoming lost in a new and all-embracing image.

In light of the Christian elements involved, the rose-garden can be seen as a place of spiritual incarnation just as readily as it can be understood as referring to some earlier, unfulfilled possibility of temporal love. Here, it comprehends both possibilities and thus serves as a fitting contemporary image of the union of the temporal and the spiritual. And it is both precise and vague, a perfect example of Eliot's "transparent language."

The "place of disaffection" of Part III of "Burnt Norton" offers another instance of how this sort of metaphorical complexity works. In the most literal sense, the place referred to is the tube, or a part of the underground railway system of London. But behind this literal level and continually maintained by it is a broad metaphorical parallel to that dark night of the soul which precedes the moment of divine union in many mystical experiences. At first, it is still the tube, the passageway in which the trains shunt back and forth, carrying their cargo of "strained time-ridden faces / Distracted from distraction by distraction" (*CP*, 120). But the human element begins to diminish, for the moment of insight cannot be

11. Smith, p. 260.

attended, "Not here / Not here the darkness, in this twittering world" (*CP*, 120). For that moment to be achieved, negation of self is required:

> Descend lower, descend only
> Into the world of perpetual solitude,
> World not world, but that which is not world,
> Internal darkness, deprivation
> And destitution of all property,
> Desiccation of the world of sense,
> Evacuation of the world of fancy,
> Inoperancy of the world of spirit.
>   (*CP*, 120–21)

The hortatory tone of this passage adds emphasis to the whole pattern of the image of subway-night. It casts up a depersonalized depiction of the way of nonattached action. The figure ends with this abrupt statement:

> This is the one way, and the other
> Is the same, not in movement
> But abstention from movement; while the world moves
> In appetency, on its metalled ways
> Of time past and time future.
>   (*CP*, 121)

The "other way" is that of meditation and contemplation, as set forth in the exercises described in the *Gita*. Both are types of approaches to illuminatory experience, but the one characterized under the metaphor of the London subway is the way of non-involved action, entered into with consciousness, but not pursued with any intensity.

The parallel between Eliot's description of this descent into the soul's dark night and the teaching of St. John of the Cross is striking. St. John marks three states of the dark night: the negation, first of the senses, then of the intellect, and ultimately of the spirit as well.[12] Eliot describes these stages with the words "desiccation," "evacuation," and "inoperancy," and the last of these is the most

12. For an extended discussion of this parallel, see Steffan Bergsten, *Time and Eternity: A Study in the Structure and Symbolism of T. S. Eliot's "Four Quartets"* (Stockholm, 1960), p. 183.

significant, for it is only when the spirit is inoperative that the grace of the divine Object can enter and permeate the soul.

A similar descent into a dark night occurs in section III of "East Coker." Most probably written against a background of what seemed like imminent destruction for England, it represents one of the most depressing and pessimistic turns in any of the four poems.[13] The warlike scene has already been set in section II, with the fight of the Sun against Scorpion taking place against a vivid backdrop of "constellated wars." Against this foreboding background, section III opens with the bleak words of Samson Agonistes, "O dark dark dark"; the destructive power of war will take all, not even leaving any for the work of burial. The people seen earlier on the London subway are here too, going nowhere from nowhere, but now they have faces and names. They are the characters of the modern world, and their names are their jobs:

The captains, merchant bankers, eminent men of letters,
The generous patrons of art, the statesmen and the rulers,
Distinguished civil servants, chairmen of many committees,
Industrial lords and petty contractors. . . .   (*CP*, 126)

The empty pomposity of these figures is emphasized by the long, heavy lines—a litany of boredom. It is a repetition, in a different key, of the refrain from "Burnt Norton" and the repetition is pointed out: "You say I am repeating / Something I have said before. I shall say it again" (*CP*, 127). So both the extended metaphors in which humans descend into two earthly "dark nights" are repeated: the first one the dark night of "tumid apathy" where masses move in and out of the subway as it scuttles through the tube, the second the dark night of war, of manmade death and destruction.

Section IV of "East Coker" opens with what Helen Gardner calls a "poem on the Passion."[14] But it is more than that, for the Passion has been translated under the metaphor of a hospital, with Christ

13. Donald Gallup, *T. S. Elliot: A Bibliography* (New York, 1953). "Burnt Norton" was first published in April 1936, in *Collected Poems 1909–1935. The Family Reunion, Old Possum's Book of Practical Cats,* and *The Idea of a Christian Society* were published between that date and May 23, 1940, when "East Coker" first appeared in *The New English Weekly Easter Number* (*Supplement*). It is fair to assume, then, that the writing of most of "East Coker" took place somewhere in the intervening period and closer to the date of its first appearance than to the date of the first issue of "Burnt Norton."

14. P. 25.

represented by the "wounded surgeon." It is Christ's action in antici-
pating the sacrificial act of Atonement for every individual which
"[resolves] the enigma of the fever chart" and brings redemptive life
to those who "obey the dying nurse" (CP, 127). This prayerful
section brings together the earlier passages which have St. John of
the Cross at their center and replaces that figure with an image of
Christ, who is both Subject and Object in the progress of the soul
toward divine insight.

The whole of the first four sections of "The Dry Salvages" functions as an extended metaphor, set in the dramatic context of the
sea and river of the beginning of the poem. The personae of the
metaphor are the fishermen of section II, and the river and sea
their habitat and source of livelihood. Yet these geographical features are no more understood and controlled by the fishermen than
the world of rational perception is understood by men anywhere.
But, in their daily struggle to earn a living from the sea, the fishermen become the embodiment of the race as it constantly works to
achieve similar aims in various ways. The union of external and
internal, of God and man, gives the pattern of daily existence its
meaning and orders life toward a destination. The union of man
and God renders all history meaningful, for it reconciles the "death
of living" with each experience of that death.

"Only the hardly, barely prayable / Prayer of the one Annunciation" answers "the voiceless wailing" and the "withering of withered
flowers, / . . . the movement of pain that is painless and motionless,"
and the "bone's prayer to Death its God" (CP, 132). Here, the fishermen recall the Fisher King of The Waste Land but they have now
become apostles, fishers of men, as well. Their daily routing, half-
understood and filled with toil, becomes an image of the religious
pattern of work-sacrifice-redemption. Thus, the metaphor relates
them to the race and their toiling-ground to the world of human
endeavor at large. The prayer they offer to the Lady at the beginning of section IV is only prayable once they have accepted the
necessity for action described in section III. Once the fact of the
Annunciation is asserted and accepted, then action becomes a
Christian imperative, even though it be left to others to turn the
products of a life to effective use. The fishermen who are able to
pray to the "Lady, whose shrine stands on the promontory" recognize their commitment to a life of action, action which is expressed
in the repetitive pattern of their daily lives.

In "Little Gidding" this pattern of sacrifice-redemption is brought full circle under the metaphor of the king's visit to a chapel at night-fall. The king, who, on one level of understanding, is Charles I, is also associated with Christ. Charles, and the rest of England's past, cannot be revived, but they have left something more signifi-cant than the hope of their revival. They have left a symbol, one which has been "perfected in death." And that symbol, seen in terms of its having Christ as its center, means no more nor less than, in words paraphrased from the *Shewings* of Juliana of Nor-wich, that "All manner of thing shall be well / By the purification of the motive / In the ground of our beseeching" (*CP*, 143). This, coming as it does near the end of the *Quartets*, is an assertion that the limits of knowing marked by the Atonement are those which must suffice for most of us. The impossible union is figured as the Incarnation, "The hint half guessed, the gift half understood, is Incarnation. / Here the impossible union / Of spheres of existence is actual, / Here the past and future / Are conquered, and reconciled" (*CP*, 136). Achieving this union is reserved for those few who are saints:

> For most of us, this is the aim
> Never here to be realised;
> Who are only undefeated
> Because we have gone on trying;
> We, content at the last
> If our temporal reversion nourish
> (Not too far from the yew-tree)
> The life of significant soil.
>   (*CP*, 136–37)

This is the nature of the "good life" as Reilly describes it to Celia in *The Cocktail Party*. People who accept the conditions of the world, who live in it but not exclusively of it, may remember

> The vision they have had, but they cease to regret it,
> Maintain themselves by the common routine,
> Learn to avoid excessive expectation,
> Become tolerant of themselves and others,
> Giving and taking, in the usual actions
> What there is to give and take.
>   (*CP*, 363–64)

Celia cannot accept this life; she aspires to the condition of the saint. For her, a life of separation, self-denial, and loneliness is the only alternative. Reilly points out to her that such a course, taken with awareness and entered into with conviction, will lead to spiritual illumination and fulfillment. She embodies, by taking that course, the life given to the saint in the *Quartets*. It is the "best life" but only a few can attain it, for it implies renouncing the things of this world and devoting oneself to a life of contemplation and self-denial.

Words are all the poet has to attempt to express this goal, and in each of the poems in the *Quartets* save one there is a passage devoted exclusively to the problem of making words equal to the task. All these passages occur in the same place, section V of each poem, and their place in the structure makes it clear they are more than digression. Eliot is burdened with the sense of the inadequacy of language and the burden is one he shares with all writers of religious poetry. "Words move, music moves / Only in time; but that which is only living / Can only die. Words, after speech, reach / Into the silence" (*CP*, 121). Words have to respect temporal and spatial rules, they have to be given human arrangement. But placed in patterns, and then repeated in patterns, they may become secondary to the design they order and the reader may be left with only the purity of the design: "Only by the form, the pattern, / Can words or music reach / The stillness, as a Chinese jar still / Moves perpetually in its stillness" (*CP*, 121). But the effect is achieved at great expense, for words "strain, / Crack and sometimes break, under the burden, / Under the tension, skip, slide, perish, / Decay with imprecision, will not stay in place, / Will not stay still" (*CP*, 121). But the effort may be worthwhile, for once words can be made to say something, the movement of time and memory has been changed and "one has only learnt to get the better of words / For the thing one no longer has to say, or the way in which / One is no longer disposed to say it" (*CP*, 128). The only word which can serve the need is the Word itself, and in "The Dry Salvages" where one might expect the passage on language we have instead the affirmation of Incarnation, the "hint half guessed, the gift half understood" (*CP*, 136).

With that recognition, the poet can claim, in the appropriate section of the last of the *Quartets*, that "What we call the beginning is often the end / And to make an end is to make a beginning" (*CP*,

144). The assertion that the "poetry does not matter" (*CP*, 125) does not, then, mean that poetry is either impossible or that it is a waste of effort, but rather that as poetry it is of little use unless it can point to something in experience which has nothing to do with poetry as such. For Eliot, poetry must suggest that not words but the Word is of vital and redemptive value. With the humility that this recognition brings, the poet can then claim also that the "beginning is often the end" and can also order words in the confidence that while saints may reach beyond language, the poet does not need to try, for the fact of Incarnation is first of all a matter of the here and now, and Christ is daily crucified and daily resurrected. If he would imitate Christ, the poet must write about the here and now. "[H]istory is a pattern / Of timeless moments. So, while the light fails / On a winter's afternoon, in a secluded chapel / History is now and England" (*CP*, 144–45).

Thus, when language is understood to be a substantial entity in a world of objects, all of them upheld and maintained by the "Love and the voice of this Calling," the struggle of the poet is redeemed, and he can say that

<blockquote>
every phrase
And sentence that is right (where every word is at home,
Taking its place to support the others,
The word neither diffident nor ostentatious,
An easy commerce of the old and the new,
The common word exact without vulgarity,
The formal word precise but not pedantic,
The complete consort dancing together)
Every phrase and every sentence is an end and a beginning,
Every poem an epitaph.   (*CP*, 144)
</blockquote>

In the final analysis, it is clear that language cannot be made to express the ineffable. But the failure is unavoidable, for the poet's vocation is to treat contingent human circumstances. One of the central themes Eliot comes to express in the *Quartets* is that language, like history, is an aspect of immediate experience. At the beginning of his career as poet, Eliot doubted that language could even accomplish the traditional task of recording one's perception of the external, phenomenal world. But gradually, as he worked his way out of that dilemma posed by his Romantic predecessors and pointed up for him so clearly in the philosophical investigations of F. H. Bradley, Eliot modified his notion that language is but an extension of the private mind and, in time, adopted a very old conception of the nature and function of words. Through the continued struggle of trying "to learn to use words," the constant "raid on the inarticulate" (*CP*, 128), Eliot discovers that by careful arrangement and conscious patterning, language can in fact communicate the objects of the contemplative mind, even when those objects are beyond the reach of empirical verification. In short, it can describe immediate experience and it can be ordered so as to suggest that that experience is a proper analogue to the experience of "things unseen." Language can (as it does in the *Quartets*) shape and define the experience of contemplation itself. In its role as offering-of-experience, language becomes a gesture, sacramental because it is offering, poetry because it is patterned. That Eliot is finally able to shape his (for our time) uncommon experience into a concrete poetry is justification enough for recognizing his as the major poetic voice of the first half of the twentieth century. That he spent a lifetime agonizing over language, that "shabby equipment always deteriorating / In the general mess of imprecision of feeling" (*CP*, 128), and learning that the trouble lies not with language but with the "imprecision" of our feeling is sufficient reason to place him in the great tradition of major Western poets. After all, they have been all of them men perplexed by the distance which separates words from deeds. Paradoxically, Eliot is finally most akin to those for whom he had the greatest distaste. Like that of both Blake and Shelley, his best poetry contains an implicit recognition that there "are indeed, things that cannot be put into words." Language is finally accepted by Eliot as being contingent, limited by its human origins and able therefore only to *point* towards "what is mystical."[15] Though perhaps from the perspective of the saint the "poetry does not matter," from that of the poet it is absolutely necessary, the only useful evidence of "the trying" which is "neither gain nor loss."

15. Wittgenstein, *Tractatus*, p. 151.

UNIVERSITY OF FLORIDA MONOGRAPHS

Humanities